AUTHORITY,
ACCOUNTABILITY,
AND THE
APOSTOLIC
MOVEMENT

AUTHORITY,
ACCOUNTABILITY,
AND THE
APOSTOLIC
MOVEMENT

DR. STEPHEN CROSBY

Pleasant Word

A Division of WINEPRESS PUBLISHING

All Scripture references are taken from the King James Bible. Public domain.

John Calvin's *Institutes of the Christian Religion*. Public domain.

Apostolic and Prophetic Foundations by Donald Rumble © 1996. Used by permission.

Who is Your Covering? by Frank Viola © 2001 Present Testimony Ministry. Used by permission.

Beyond All Limits by Bill Bright and James O. Davies. © 2000. New Life Publications, Orlando, FL. Used by permission. All rights reserved.

Churchquake by Peter Wagner © 1999 Regal Books, Ventura, CA 93003. Used by permission

Apostles and the Emerging Apostolic Movement by David Cannistraci © 1996 Regal Books, Ventura, CA 93003. Used by permission.

Reprinted by Permission. *Under Cover* by John Bevere, © 2001, Thomas Nelson, Inc. Nashville, Tennessee, All rights reserved.

Listening to the Spirit in the Text by Gordon Fee. Grand Rapids: Eerdmans, 2000, and the NIV *Commentary on the New Testament, The First Epistle to the Corinthians, by Gordon Fee*. Grand Rapids: Eerdmans, 1987. Used by Permission. All rights reserved.

Apostolic Strategies Affecting Nations by Jonathan David, © 1997, Self-published. Used by permission.

ISBN 1-4141-0640-8
Library of Congress Catalog Card Number: 2005911076

ENDORSEMENTS

Oh, where was this book when I was in seminary!? As the fourth in a spiritual lineage of shipwrecked preachers, with personal testimony to the life-threatening impact brought on by the stress of living with a faulty understanding of authority and control in the church, I have one thing to say: better late than never! Thanks so much, Steve, for this insightful and understandable book.

This book is a must read for all Christians.

—Pastor Chris Savino, Wasilla, AK

When you get right down to it, the theme of the gospel is amazingly simple: crucifixion and resurrection. Those ideals were modeled in Christ, and if He is truly the center of our actions, they should be replayed in all we do. It is so easy to forget these simple things and build kingdoms that are of men rather than God. Steve takes us back to the correct central theme of the gospel. The teaching and ministry of apostles and prophets should reflect the correct gospel foundation. Has the new apostolic reformation succeeded in this mandate? Or has it been the vehicle used to build the kingdoms of men? This book probes these issues and questions. It can potentially bring great freedom to not only those who consider themselves apostles or prophets but also to every Christian who may have wandered from the simplicity of the gospel.

—Pastor Jim Brittain, Talkeetna, AK

Reading this book is like stopping at a scenic overlook. It causes everything to take on new and fresh beauty that we couldn't have imagined before. Much of what Steve shares in this book is in sharp contrast and confrontation to the status quo. It's startling enough to make your eyes pop open wide and cause you to exclaim, "That's it! That's the truth!" This book breathes new life into the biblical landscape of authority and submission. During the last several years, I have observed Pastor Steve pour out his heart and soul to bring maturity to the body of Christ in the US, the Philippines, and in Great Britain. His concern has not been for his own needs but to truly connect believers with Christ, their Life-Source. He then quietly steps away and lets the life flow. This book is written in that same spirit.

—Kevin Stafford, Walla Walla, WA

I can't say it any simpler than this. Steve Crosby gets it. His insight into the Apostolic Reformation Movement answers many questions and provides an appropriate and balanced contrast to prevailing "apostolic" philosophies. This kind of biblical approach is what the church needs. It provides the understanding and ability to close the gap that has existed between "us" and "them," the leadership and the laity, those who submit and those to whom others submit, the apostle and the Christian "everyman."

—Michael Cannon, Spokane, WA

Authority, Accountability, and the Apostolic Movement arrives at exactly the right time during God's restoration of the apostolic to His church. The maturing of every kingdom move requires rigorous recognition of human excess without reactive rejection of godly essence. Steve Crosby draws from his experience as an author, senior pastor, and prophetic teacher to pull off this divine balance. I heartily recommend it to all leaders, regardless of their present doctrinal position on the apostolic.

—Pastor Alan Corrick, Fairbanks, AK

There are movements and understandings which have come into Christianity at various times throughout its history: some of these new insights might be called "present truth" or "recovered truth." These new paradigms are useful to the church in knowing how to operate more according to the will of God in the present circumstances. Often, however, after a time, the human element enters in and what had been at first "illuminating" and freeing to the body of Christ becomes domineering and arbitrarily binding upon the conscience of Christian men and women. It is always a dangerous trend when such a movement labels any critique of its methods as "opposed to the present day work of the Holy Spirit" and against what God wants to do through certain leaders. This blurs the line for many between what is truly of God and human hubris. Adherents "fear" to oppose or even not to support these views lest they be "opposing God." It will often take a sharp critique from within to bring balance to any movement which has gone to this extreme in insulating itself from rational and/or spiritual evaluation.

Dr. Crosby's analysis of the present day "Apostolic Movement" will undoubtedly draw some fire; but I hope that many will at least listen and hear what the Lord may be saying through this book in order that we as the body of Christ may "get it right," not "not throwing out the baby with the bathwater," but at least recognizing what in the end should be thrown out—"impure waters" not meant for repeated use.

—Dr. William Suttles, Director
Raleigh Institute of Biblical Studies
Raleigh, NC

Steve Crosby has a powerful and succinct way of expressing himself. In this book he has aimed this powerful weapon on a specific target - the current "apostolic" movement. However, his salvos also illuminated a much bigger issue. In explaining the scriptural reasons why there is error in this particular movement, he had to address a much wider issue - the fact that the New Covenant is a better covenant than the Old Covenant. We all know this - or do we? Crosby shows that many New Testament believers have an Old Testament mindset, are in bondage because of it, and have no idea this is the root of their problems.

Every Christian who continually falls short in their walk with the Lord, and wonders why, should read this book. It is quite possible that they will discover the reason for their frustration and impotence

—Edward Kurath
Divinely Designed Ministries
Post Falls, ID

TABLE OF CONTENTS

FOREWORD

This book is going to cause an explosion!

The Scripture teaches that two identifying marks of a wise master builder in God's house are that he lays the foundation and that he then releases others to build on it (1 Corinthians 3:10).

1. He lays the proper foundation: that foundation can only be Jesus Christ Himself (1 Corinthians 3:11). Everything we do in the local church must depend upon Him. We listen for what He is saying; we follow Him in what He is doing. We do not gather to Him as He is interpreted to us through a few gifted leaders; we gather to Him as the Holy Spirit reveals Him through whomever He chooses. Leaders then oversee the process of a functioning body of believers who are being trained to hear and respond to Christ their Head.

2. Believers other than the apostle must be released to build upon the foundation. When apostolic men build churches into a dependence upon themselves, they are either not apostolic in a New Testament sense or they are not wise. Paul was both.

Today the church faces a serious debate. How do we build in such a way that true apostolic authority is recognized and received while at the same time Christ's body is released to function in all the diversity of God's abiding grace? Steve Crosby takes this formidable challenge head on in *Authority, Accountability, and the Apostolic Movement.*

Readers be warned: this book will confront widely-held beliefs and wisely seek to persuade you that apostolic authority is about keeping believers "Christ-aligned" not "apostle-aligned." While Steve and I hold some differing views, I believe this book will help to set free many who have been wounded by often well-meaning but misguided men seeking to build in an apostolic way.

—DON RUMBLE
www.csnbooks.com/rumble

PREFACE

"Danger! Danger! Warning, Will Robinson!"[1]

This text will be controversial for some. My friends have warned me it is crosscurrent with the dominant trend in charismatic literature on the subject. I know that. Misrepresentation is a chance I must take. I believe in apostles, prophets, authority, submission, and leadership. However, I believe the published theology and practiced methods of what is emerging on the topic are deeply and dangerously flawed.

The failure to preach and apply these topics with cultural sensitivities,[2] a thorough understanding of the New Covenant, and the implications of the indwelling Spirit in humanity since Pentecost makes a spiritual chiropractic treatment an urgent need. Passive self-adjustment over time will not fix the problem. Crooked things do not tend to correct themselves as time progresses. Straightening requires pressure and usually the earlier the better. As we learned from Isaac Newton, once something gets going and picks up steam, it takes a lot of energy to stop it. The apostolic train has left the station, it has gone around a couple of turns, and is picking up momentum. Unfortunately, a few passengers and their luggage have been unnecessarily lost on the last two high-speed curves, and a mile ahead the bridge is out. Someone needs to send a warning.

If you have ever been around a reformed alcoholic or a former smoker, you may have noticed that tact can suffer at the hands of passion. This is always the reformer's dilemma: when to apply pressure and when to back off. One of the dangers readers will face herein is misinterpreting my passion for Christ as reaction to personal history and wounding. I can only state in honesty before the Lord, I am not writing from woundedness. However, I am aware, that when the Lord was passing out spiritual gift packages, I was not in the diplomacy queue!

As many of our dear friends know, that accompanied by a burst of faith-filled positive confession, Rita's and my experience in the church could be called an "adventure." In less cheery moments, it could be called a bad dream, and when hopelessly aligned with the devil, you might call it a nightmare! Rita defines the difference between a bad dream and a nightmare like this: in the former you are in pain, in the latter there is blood on the floor and you are missing a few limbs! Well, we have all our appendages, but we do carry a few battle scars. Hopefully, they are honorable in His cause.

Indeed, our path in God has been interesting. No one with three grams of brain matter left in his head would ever want or choose our path—but for the call and grace of God. Indeed, our first years of church experience were abusive. We could easily take the gold in the authority abuse Olympics, and set a few records in the process! We will spare you the details, as we long ago forgave and are over it. The last eighteen years have been at times colorful, confusing, painful, weird, and wonderful, but not abusive. Some of our friends have suggested we write a story of our lives. I would except that reading it would run afoul of the constitution's prohibition against cruel and unusual punishment and no one would believe it anyway! I don't think there is a literary marketing genre that covers "Christian Horror" – it is a tough sell.

Be that as it may, we have survived the worst that humanity in the church has to offer. We are not bitter, *still love* the Lord (in all His glory),

His church (in all its forms), *and* her leaders (in all their weaknesses). This says something about God's unmerited preserving power. I am aware that there are many shipwrecked souls whose faith is no longer in one piece who, for some reason, have not weathered church experience with the same grace. Words are inadequate to express how deeply I "feel their pain." We can't explain why we survived, but we did and we are thankful for it. We are determined to rescue and spare as many as we can from clumsy mishandling within God's own church.

The reason for our colorful journey is God's great redemptive purpose to use our pain to save others from it. That is the essence of the Incarnation and the essence of Christianity. Pain no longer happens in a vacuum. It has redemptive purpose. Our desire is to redeem those already in abusive environments and to prevent others from following suit into one. What good is any of our pain if we cannot learn from it?

This is my/our passion in writing: passion for the preeminence of Christ and an aching desire to see others spared. If tragedy does not move us there is something wrong. It is difficult to watch as abusive authority doctrines and practices espoused as the new apostolic revelation emerge and shipwreck the lives and faith of thousands. If my reformer's zeal gets the best of me from time to time, well, at least you will know what is going on. It is a passionate matter.

When teachings that proclaim themselves the "new apostolic revelation" or the "new apostolic order" supplant Christ's unique person, place, and work, betray the New Covenant, put millions of believers into bondage to a corrupt manmade system, persist and expand, *something must be said*. Paul was passionate concerning the supplanting of Christ. I am keenly aware of my own deficiencies and inadequacies. I also understand I am not the doctrinal sheriff for the body of Christ. However, I am an unapologetic defender of Christ's uniqueness and preeminence against angel, demon, king, prophet, pastor, apostle, or Christian celebrity who espouse such doctrines.

This book is also not about pointing out what everyone else is doing wrong. That is an exercise in futility. I write with familiarity and passion on the subject because of what was done to us by leaders, and sadly, what I have done to others as a leader. Over the years as a leader, I taught some of the doctrines critiqued herein. I would not want to listen to my own messages from fifteen years ago! At one level, that is good, because all of us grow in grace and our understanding of our Lord, His Word, and His ways. So while I truly regret some of what I taught in the past, I trust that God's sovereign redemptive grace really does work everything together for good (even the garbage we leaders sometimes dump on people!) for those that love Him and are the called according to His purpose. Someone once told me that churches deserve the pastors they get and pastors deserve the congregations they get. I don't know how theologically accurate that is, but it does have a sovereign ring about it, and with a few decades of historical perspective under the belt, often seems to approximate reality.

Before we launch ahead, I have one more interpretive lens I would like to provide the reader. The love of God[3] is expressed through one's calling and gift mix.[4] A pastor/shepherd expresses love through care. An evangelist expresses love through hope and encouragement. A teacher expresses love through instruction. Books written by pastor/teachers and books written by prophet/apostles (or apostle/prophets) are fundamentally different. Typically when a pastor writes a book, it will be warm and encouraging with lots of stories and life-application truths. It will provide a general sense of well being when read. That is fine. That is what the pastoral anointing is supposed to do. However, this book is not pastoral but prophetic and apostolic in nature. Let me explain. It might go easier for you!

A prophet expresses love through the removal of idolatrous and false structures that keep God's people in blind bondage. A prophet calls God's people to alignment with the divine plumb line of truth.[5] Prophets bring the immediacy of God. It is part of their calling to bring people face to face with issues they can no longer ignore. To be prophetic is to nurture, nourish, and evoke a consciousness and perception that is alternative to the consciousness and perception of the dominant environment around us,[6] whatever that environment might be. Specifically, prophets evoke a Christ-consciousness in folks who do not normally realize that they ever had one or that they have lost it.

That is inherently confrontational and aligning. In our therapeutic, feel-good, self-centered, bless-me, American church culture, the prophetic voice is routinely marginalized or silenced under the guise of it being divisive or not conducive to unity—it upsets too many people. The prophetic anointing is considered by some as "unloving." Prophets do not bring the sauna and massage anointing to the church. They bring the chiropractic anointing to the church! In a culture that is dominated with a pastoral ethos, this is often misread as being "in your face" and some how inappropriate. Well, that's what prophets do! Prophets are always a threat to established systems. Being prophetic is not a disorder that needs to be fixed; it is a voice that needs to be listened to. Not necessarily agreed with but listened to.

This book is also apostolic in nature. Part of being apostolic is similar to the prophetic function in that apostles have concern for the primacy of Christ's person and His gospel. Apostles, in part, are concerned that God's people might correctly apprehend Christ for who He is through an unveiling act of the Holy Spirit. There is something about "spiritual accuracy" that is fundamentally reforming and part of the fiber of an apostolic anointing. Reforming something means moving it from where it wants to be to where it should be. Whether it is straightening teeth or crooked doctrine, it takes pressure. You will feel it.

Being foundational-building ministries, both the apostolic and prophetic anointings are concerned about the accuracy of divine alignment in the foundation. You cannot afford tilt in the foundation. Everything that follows will tilt also. Therefore, the apostolic is also a "chiropractic" anointing. It is not an issue of being accurately aligned to the apostle, the person, or the ministry but through an apostolic anointing being accurately aligned with the only true and reliable Cornerstone, Christ Jesus.

So if this book is genuinely apostolic and prophetic in nature, you will get a lovely double dose of spiritual alignment. You will "feel it" throughout. That is OK. That's what you should feel. We will try to tell a distracting joke or two just before we snap your neck. You will survive. God will see to it that you get a nice follow-up pastoral sauna and massage with an angelic cabana boy to help your recovery.

I have deep respect and admiration for those scholars whose life labors I so easily avail myself of by turning my chair toward my multi-volume library or by a click of a mouse. However, this work is not intended to meet the rigors of academia. Rather, my passion is for practical concerns particularly as they relate to the alarming trends emerging in the so-called apostolic renewal or reformation movement of the current hour.

I desire to "re-present" theology to the church in a way that is digest-ible and applicable to local church leaders and believers. However, the intricacies of the issue require consideration of biblical interpretation, exegesis, original languages, word definitions, etc. that some readers may find hard chewing, perhaps even tedious or belaboring. I ask that the nonacademic reader please persist and trust that the Holy Spirit will witness to what is true and necessary and negate that which is not. I hope this text not only sparks healthy debate but also provides a measure of divine alignment to what I believe in and have given my life for: the present-day reality and function of apostles and prophets.

I am also aware that in an antiauthority and individualistic culture such as the USA (the West in general) misuse and abuse of the view presented herein is a risk. However, I believe it is worth it. Misuse of personal freedom at the hands of self-willed believers is certainly no worse than the misuse of authority by insecure leaders on the other end of the spectrum. The Spirit is not asleep on the job. He is always pressing the pendulum in us, one way or the other, until we reach that Day.

ACKNOWLEDGEMENTS

I would like to thank my wife, Rita, my family, and all my friends and fellow laborers around the world for their love and support. A man's true riches are defined by his relationships, not his wallet. You have made me a wealthy man.

Thank you to the fine leaders and family of God at New Life Covenant Church in Wasilla, AK whose kind generosity enabled me to have unencumbered time to write this work.

My special thanks go to my entire editorial review team but especially Mr. Kevin Stafford for bringing his exceptional gifts and talents to bear on this effort.

INTRODUCTION

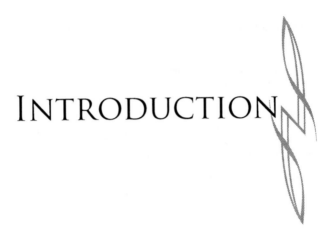

God's Word has been my daily bread for thirty years. Since my conversion, appetite for Him in the Word has been a resident blessing. The older I grow in God, the more I am convinced of several "principles" related to Scripture study.

David's Key

Over time, personal discipline and intellectual exercise can imperceptibly displace spiritual vitality. Without personal passion for Christ, our faith resembles a stale marriage. Maintaining legalities and obedient behavior through force of will gives the appearance of a marriage, but substance is lost. Familiarity, routine, boredom, and benign indifference produce relational alienation as effectively as a marital crisis. Warehousing biblical knowledge does not necessarily require relational intimacy. When grace no longer amazes we are merely the walking dead.

Imagine an ink dot on a balloon. The dot represents my biblical knowledge at any moment in time. The rest of the balloon's surface represents what I do not understand. If I blew up the balloon, *both* the dot and the balloon would expand. The more I know of Him, the less I know. Every step of understanding yields a mile of mystery. Mastery of precepts is finite. Relationship with a person is inexhaustible. Facts are manageable. Personality is not. Like Mary Magdalene in the garden, we may touch Him, but He will never allow us to hold Him.[1] He is eminently knowable, yet elusively beyond our grasp.

The Bible is inspired and infallible, but my understanding of it is neither. Fundamental Christendom tends to blur this line. We all, including myself, bring imperceptible biases and presuppositions to our reading of the text. This does not bother me. Those who believe themselves without bias because of a certain theological stance concern me greatly. Principles of interpretation may keep us out of the theological ditch, but they do not guarantee that we do not swerve out of our lane from time to time.

Theology is the child of worship. The Bible, or our intellectual apprehension of it, can become the object of our commitment, devotion, and worship rather than the Lord in His person. This is mental idolatry respectably dressed in the language of God's own Word. My intellect alone is insufficient to study His book.

The passkey of scriptural understanding belongs to David in type.[2] The "key of David" likely refers to issues associated with Christ's link to David in rulership.[3] However, we cannot forget that David was distinguished in his generation by a personal, living relationship with Yahweh, ahead of its time in substance and quality. The foundation of David's relationship was a lifestyle of intimacy through worship. Without individual interaction with the person of the Holy Spirit in the revelation of His Word, the Bible is a locked book. The key of hermeneutics only works in the hand of a worshiper. David's key opens. David's key closes. *No one* gets in without it.

Mountains and Molehills

If we think the Bible is a rulebook with the "answer" for every nuance of human circumstance, we have either not read it very well or lived very long! It is an exegetical, spiritual, and relational mistake to be rigid in areas where the New Covenant is either silent or open to different possibilities of interpretation. This is neither a cave-in to post-modernism nor a weakening of scriptural integrity. It is honesty—a quality that often suffers under religious insecurity and rigidity.

Spiritual rigidity is not a virtue of maturity. It is a vice when God is smaller than our intellect. Combativeness is a sign of "young manhood." Young men, naturally and spiritually, want to fight about everything.[4] Knowingness is a sign of fatherhood.[5] Fathers have learned to pick their battles. I am not advocating vacillation in core doctrine or morality—legitimate areas for leadership authority. Rather, I am urging an inner inclination that is slow to make absolutist and doctrinally binding proclamations concerning what may be scripturally legitimate but subordinate themes (elevating secondary themes to major status). The tendency to elevate something marginal to something ultimate contributes to a clinical and cold quality that is uninviting to the unbeliever and repugnant to the Lord to whom we profess allegiance. Jesus called it straining at gnats and swallowing camels.[6]

God's Elastic Band

Perceptual tension is divinely designed into God's Word. The entire book consists of principles and emphases in complementary or competing tension. Like two sides of a coin, many themes in the Word seem at first glance to be polar opposites. Skeptics, rationalists, and critics futilely mine here for fool's gold, allegedly "proving" incoherence and unreliability of the Word.

An iron bar with opposing north/south polarity is called a magnet. Remove the polarity and a magnet simply becomes a chunk of iron. Remove the polarities of God's Word and the resultant doctrinal emphases will be equally useless, if not aberrant or harmful. Every emphasis in Scripture has, to borrow a phrase from Isaac Newton, equal and opposite emphases.

Apparent contradictions disappear when we understand the principle of *antinomy*. Antinomy describes two statements, conclusions, laws, or principles that seem equally logical, reasonable, or necessary but exist in irresolvable conflict or contradiction with each other.[7]

Most heretical teaching and improper emphasis results from attempting to undo or resolve divinely designed antinomies. God's Word is like an elastic band; it only functions in tension. When considered in tension and totality, God's Word coheres. Release the tension through intellectual jockeying and no end of doctrinal strangeness will result. This is not a left or right wing, conservative or liberal, traditionalist or modernist issue. Aberrations, imbalance, over and under emphasis occur all across the Christian landscape.

What follows are four limited examples of biblical concepts that, while not antinomies in the strictest philosophical sense, have "antinomic" tension.

The Dual Nature of Christ

What is the dual nature of Christ, the God-man but an antinomic revelation explainable only through the mystery of the incarnation? Who is really able to completely explain such a Christ? Our theological forefathers made noble contributions summarized in the historical creeds and theology of the Church, but the line between heresy and orthodoxy can be painfully thin and is often determined by where one puts emphasis—His deity or manhood.

God's Love and Hate

God's love and hate are a troublesome antinomy in our psychotherapeutic Western culture. The phrase, "love the sinner, hate the sin" is a great model for interpersonal evangelism. However, it does not accurately describe God based on the totality of scriptural revelation. Psalm 11:5 says God hates the sinner: literally, with odious, personal, hatred from the depths of His being.[8] Yet the same Scriptures (John 3) say He unconditionally loves the world.[9] How can both of these be true?

Understanding that love and hate are not psychological or emotional qualities in a Semitic worldview[10] helps "resolve" this tension. So does understanding the cross of Christ as simultaneously displaying God's holy hatred toward sin and His holy love on the sinner. God is not just love. He is *holy* love.

Interpersonal Offences

How should we respond to a brother or sister who offends us or is caught in open sin? Well, the Scriptures are crystal clear. We are to cover their sin.[11] That is the manifestation of God's love, is it not? Not so fast. The same Scriptures tell us that we are to openly rebuke them.[12] Which is correct? Both and neither. This antinomic tension is relieved when we understand that He is Lord over His Word. We are responsible to be led by the Spirit, not by the Spirit's code book. If we posses the code but lose touch with the Person, we are, of all people, the most dangerous. We are supposed to be abiding in a living and vibrant relationship with Him, not merely looking to the Scriptures as "Life for Dummies" or the *Cliff Notes©* of human survival.

Yippee or Yowee

Not only do thematic tensions exist in the Word, but also how one reads the Scriptures is heavily influenced by personality, experience, and calling. This is not the same as unfaithfully mishandling it. It is just reality when human beings interact with God's eternal Word.

A friend of mind once said that people see and speak from their passion, pain, or a mixture of both. One's theological position on a subject is often the reactionary response to hurt or abuse experienced at the opposite end of the theological spectrum. When speaking from passion or pain, it is often difficult to see other equally valid but opposite passions. It is hard to appreciate another's journey. Their life experiences and life messages may not flip my switch. It may even blow my circuits.

If my personal history was one of great suffering, personal pain, sorrow, trial, and tragedy, I could be drawn to Scripture that emphasize blessedness, prosperity, and favor. This is reasonable! As a human being, I am looking for hope and relief. The content of my emphasis could be completely "biblical" and fundamentally sound—from my perspective. However, my experience might render my spiritual tuner slightly dull to those passages that speak of suffering, hardship, trial, or loss. Scriptures clearly speak of both! We can make idolatrous camps at the antinomic extremes of personal peace and affluence or monastic self-flagellation and poverty.

- In the world but not of it.
- Seated in the heavenlies but on earth.
- Dead but alive.
- Slaves but free.
- Poor yet rich.
- The kingdom present, the kingdom future.

Tension characterizes the Word from cover to cover. Christ incarnate, crucified, risen, and coming again is the revealed tension reliever.

C'mon Joe, What D'ya Really Know?

Nowhere is divine tension in Scripture more painfully clear than in the matter of submission to authority and personal freedom. One of the great themes of Scripture is God's government. From its denial in Genesis to its universal restoration in Revelation, the argument can be made that the entire canon concerns the expansion of God's rule throughout the creation.

That the government is on His (Messiah's) shoulders[13] does not raise too much theological dander. *How* Messiah's rule is delegated and implemented by imperfect human beings does. Like Goldilocks trying out the three bears' beds, the challenge is to find authority that is neither too hard nor too soft but just right. She might have difficulty getting a good night's sleep among us. The diverse forms of church government among sincere Bible believers self-attest that the Scriptures do not speak with crystal clarity on the matter. Shouting authority and submission proof texts at one another will not suffice.

As Gordon Fee points out in *Listening to the Spirit in the Text*, the Scripture speaks some about the character and ethic (1 Timothy 3; Titus 1; 1 Peter 5:3) required of church leaders, but it says nothing of structure, function, and method. "Thus, in the final analysis, we know very little about the governance of either the local or larger church.[14] We should probably all yield to the reality that there are no explicitly revealed church structures that serve as the divine order for all times and in all places.[15]"

Church history, denominational structures, and interpersonal relationships are replete with misunderstanding, division, hurt, pain, and abuse involving authority and submission issues. It is a volatile subject at the practical local church level. Authoritarian pastors abuse churches. Controlling churches (boards) abuse pastors. Horror stories on either extreme are as plentiful as potatoes in Idaho.

If you are a leader who has been hurt by the anarchy, independence, rebellion, control, manipulation, and betrayal of sheep and subordinate leaders, you will gravitate to Scripture that appears to emphasize themes like government, ruling, authority, covenant, and submission to authority. A leader's unresolved psychological issues of insecurity or control, or personality flaws add a toxic quality to what otherwise may be legitimate material. The toxicity flows from pulpit to pew.

On the other hand, if you are a "saint" (non-leader) who has been hurt by authoritarian governmental styles, you will gravitate toward Scriptures that speak of liberty, individuality, freedom, grace, and non-mediated relationship with the Lord. If latent streams of woundedness, victimization, independence, rebellion, and unteachableness flow in the veins of a saint, the toxicity flows from pew to pulpit. If damage exists in both pulpit and pew, there is no flow—just a toxic, religious swamp with everybody scrambling for psychological survival. This is, unfortunately, the most common scenario.

We are normally unable to see the legitimacy of the other's perspective. In our eyes, our view is the only "biblically-correct one." It feels so right at a psychological level. Our view seems remedial to our experience of abuse and therefore becomes the new and ultimate word to the church. Mix in some personality temperament issues and we have the makings of quite a mental stronghold. The most impenetrable strongholds are not those based on ungodly premises but rather those built from select biblical premises to the exclusion of others! Strongholds of falsehood come down relatively easily. Strongholds of imbalanced, partial, or ill-timed truth are near impregnable.

Trash or Treasure

Reactionary generational responses characterize American Protestant church history. Treasure in one generation is trash in the next. New order believers are convinced they bring divine adjustment, and the old-guard faithful believe compromise encroaches upon the ancient landmark. The new order believers tend to be a bit aggressive, and the old guards are unable to let go of what they have invested in. Change is one of the few constants in the kingdom. The kingdom is inherently a transforming, constantly reforming kingdom. Old-guard values must pass through death and resurrection to be generationally renewed in vitality. Unfortunately, the death and resurrection process feels a lot like a one-way toss into the dumpster. That is the thing about death: it is death—too much to face alone without faith's hope.

If the old guard expects the resurrection harvest to resemble the seed that was sown, they are in for a big disappointment. Resurrection, by definition, is an act of loss, transformation, rebirth, and multiplication, not duplication and reproduction. Cloning results in multiplication of the status quo. Death and resurrection is a transformational change of order, not merely reproduction and expansion of what has been. What is raised bears no resemblance to what was sown. It has the same DNA but not identical image. This phenomenon can play out multiple times in the life of a local church as well as globally in the Church Universal.

In this work, I hope to avoid reactionary extremes. I am aiming for the radical middle. The radical middle is not static, it is fluid: at times moderate and at times radical. Those with polar inclinations often view the middle as the safety zone for cowards! I have heard it said that the only things in the middle of the road are yellow lines and dead skunks. Let's hope that is a "limited metaphor!" The radical middle is hardly safe. It means folks at both ends of the spectrum are going to be unhappy with you!

We need a practical theology of authority that is faithful to the character and nature of God in Christ. The Calvary Act, the New Covenant, the new creation order, the spirit, sweep, and scope of the entire counsel of Scripture must illumine our understanding, not merely a biblical few proof texts, one way or the other.

My concern is not the thematic presence of government or authority and submission, neither in Scripture nor in the current apostolic renewal.[16] Rather, my objection is the alleged need for every believer to be "under an apostolic covering" and other derivative teachings related to an allegedly "restored" apostolic governmental order. My issues are:

- Distortion of legitimate biblical themes and unbalanced emphasis (making a minor a major)
- Our methods of implementation and application regarding authority and submission
- Our motives in asking for submission and the motives in those who so readily comply
- Our expectations, procedural and emotional, of what submission yields
- Our understanding of what the essence of godly authority really is

Authority, Accountability, and the Apostolic Movement

The argument might be put forward that these matters should be left alone, that as life emerges, it is messy, and given time, it will self-correct. My premise is that the teaching of apostolic covering (and related topics) is not a benign, undeveloped, immature revelation. It is a corrupt perversion and resurrected form of distorted discipleship teaching. A weed is best pulled before its root system develops. The weed must be pulled—*now!*

PART 1

The View from Thirty Thousand Feet

CHAPTER 1

CHARTING THE COURSE

I t is a mistake to begin an unfamiliar journey without a map, even though males may be genetically predisposed to try anyway! In this book we will be sailing the swells and troughs of the technical language details concerning authority, submission, obedience, headship, covering, rulership, leadership, the set man,[1] etc. Old maps are not sufficient to sail in these shifting definitional shoals. Footing may be precarious. It may be a challenging ride. The security and familiarity of shore can be very appealing when I sense my long-held personal convictions being lost into the rough sea of unfamiliar terms. The trip's necessity and belief in a safe route must reside in us, or the first time we feel our theological lunch shifting in our stomachs, we will chart a course for home—lickety-split.

In the pre-politically-correct era, before self-esteem became a national obsession, there used to be a dog food manufacturer whose commercial jingle went: "My dog's bigger than your dog, my dog's bigger than yours. My dog's bigger, 'cuz he eats ————, my dog's bigger than yours." If we approach this topic on who has the biggest concordance, we are not going to get too far, and the politically-correct thought police will rap our spiritual knuckles. Our view must be larger than the columns of a concordance alone. It must be more than what dueling definitions can provide. Before we sail the seas of easily misnavigated doctrinal waters concerning authority in the church, a global framework is required.

Believers with extensive local church background tend to process thought through the grid of previous experience (especially sensitive or painful) and training. This is essentially neither good nor bad, but it can limit what the Spirit is able to reach us with. There is a Spirit dynamic of s-t-r-e-t-c-h[2] that is not always welcome in the community of faith. A friend of mine likes to ask Christians this question: *"If what you believe to be true today would turn out to be wrong tomorrow, would you want to know today so you could change your thinking?"* Unfortunately, a high percentage of responders reply in the negative. We will usually choose the security of familiar error over the uncertain implications of new perspectives. This happens when a Christian's trust is in his/her understanding of the Scripture rather than the person of Christ.

Change is threatening. Because Christianity at its core deals with ultimate and absolute issues, processing change is difficult. Changing one's view becomes the abandonment of perceived absolute principles (that we taught and endorsed in the past) rather than ongoing development of understanding into[3] a Person—necessary for spiritual maturity and growth in Christ. Change is intellectually, spiritually, emotionally, psychologically, and organizationally unnerving. It requires we admit we may have been wrong. Teachers may have to repent for what was taught yesterday. Learners may have to forgive. Organizations and administrations whose existence requires the maintenance of historical positions and views will fight for their life when presented with understanding that may call their legitimacy into question. Change is not easy for any of us.

With these introductory guidelines in mind, let's chart a course through some of the shoals and reefs underlying much of what is taught in the church concerning authority and submission, particularly as it relates to, in at least some charismatic circles, the emergent apostolic movement[4] and the doctrine of spiritual covering.

Mapping God's Governmental Order

It is often taught that one function of an apostle, if not *the* primary function (we will deal with Titus 1:5 later in this text), is to establish God's governmental order in the church.[5] It is assumed that if God's order of things is discovered, recovered, and implemented God will release His otherwise withheld blessings.[6] Failure to come into divine order and "governmental alignment" allegedly withholds God's full order of blessing on the individual believer and in the church and puts the believer in grave spiritual jeopardy.[7] A related teaching states that part of the necessary governmental restoration is the recovery of apostles to their place of appropriate honor, authority, function, and office. The full blessing of God and spiritual protection is believed to be literally brokered to individuals and the church through the restored "covering" of the apostolic office (and variations of this theme).[8] It is also alleged that the apostle is the chief of the Ephesians 4:11–13 ministries, if not in a formal hierarchical and governmental way, at least in an informal and relational way.

A common anecdotal teaching used to explain this alleged divine order is that of the hand/fingers/thumbs.[9] The thumb is said to represent the apostle, and the other Ephesians 4:11 ministries are the fingers. Since the thumb can readily touch each of the other four fingers, but not vice versa, so supposedly the office of apostle is superior (in some way—rank, function, authority) to the other ministries. The other ministries are to assume a subordinate or submissive posture toward the apostle. Now this analogy may be clever, but it is completely without biblical exegetical support. Many things that may charmingly float homiletically[10] will not withstand close biblical scrutiny. The problem is self-inflicted by prejudicially defining the apostolic in terms of government and ruling rather than love and service.

What exactly *is* God's governmental order? What is it characterized by? How is it implemented? What is its expression? These questions and more need to be examined from a New Covenant perspective.

True North

> Verily, verily, I say unto you, Except a corn of wheat fall into the ground and die, it abideth alone: but if it die, it bringeth forth much fruit.
>
> (John 12:24)

God's kingdom does not experience increase as the result of a recovered order of things. It does not grow by the careful management and placement of subordinate theological pieces—whatever they may be. The fundamental premise that a recovered apostolic order is necessary for full kingdom life runs afoul of the most basic premise of New Covenant life: the kingdom grows, and blessing is released, through death and resurrection. Where the spirit of resurrection life is manifest, it is annoyingly surprising how much blessing flows among disorder!

Corinth was not only in disorder, but also in moral and doctrinal chaos. Yet blessing was flowing. Galatia was in extreme disorder, on the verge of apostasy, and blessing was flowing. Thessalonica was in doctrinal disorder and blessing was flowing. Colossae was in doctrinal disorder and blessing was flowing. The point is not "do apostles bring order?" Of course they do. The apostolic-prophetic heart is ever-increasing movement toward conformity to the image of Christ individually and conformity to the divine plumb line corporately. The issue is making God's blessing *contingent* on maintaining relationship to an individual apostle as a covering or the achievement of divine order as the *prerequisite* for blessing. That is error. Imperfection and movement toward order simultaneously coexist. They always have and they always will. The wheat and the tares will exist until the end of the age. God's blessing is not withheld because of a lack of order. He is not after our perfected operational systems and organizational charts. He is after our hearts. He will work with, and bless, the most imperfect presentation offered to Him. The pure in heart, not the most perfectly ordered, will see (understand, get insight, etc.) God.[11]

If in the Old Covenant dispensation God used the chaotic lives of individuals with glaring deficiencies in morals, thought, and action, how much more so should it be in the New Covenant based on better promises and the shed blood of the Lamb of God?[12] The New Covenant is not a covenant of systematic perfections and order. It is about the perfections of the resurrected life of the Son of God, manifested in mortal flesh.

Inherent in the contingent blessing and recovered order mindset is a legal spirit of perfectionism and qualified grace: "If we just get things right enough, God will come through in greater measure than we have known." In this premise, humanity's obedience conditions God's initiation. A dubious proposition, if true, that at best begs this question: *How much obedience must we produce in order to release the blessing?* How much has to be "in order" and aligned governmentally to qualify for the supposed release of the Spirit? If the blessing follows the alleged alignment, then we have merited it by our correctness of form. This thinking is idealism and perfectionism contrary to the spirit of gospel grace. The truth is, none of us will ever be "right enough" in motive, spirit, expression, or form to merit God's blessing. *Our obedience is the fruit of God's blessing, not the root of His blessing.*[13] Of course, we need to pursue order and bring our churches in to order. We need His blessing in order to do so. We do not earn His blessing because we have accomplished it.

Christ's government increases and expands because it is eternal in nature through death and resurrection life. Resurrection is the quality of eternality introduced into space and time. Life, by definition, is expansive—it grows and spreads. The Spirit at Pentecost "impregnated" the cosmos, the earth, with resurrection-life Seed. His government increases *wherever* the Seed springs up into expression, regardless of our order, structure, and forms. To teach, emphasize, or build governmental authority structures apart from a thorough understanding, and practical expression of, death and resurrection is like putting a magnet next to a compass. It becomes a false center and will lead you astray. There is only one lodestar of the kingdom: Christ and Him crucified.

Working on the Apostolic Plantation

Scripture (and much pulpit preaching) refers to the ministry of an apostle metaphorically as a "father" (1 Corinthians 4:15). Some assert that a father-son relationship is part of God's universal governmental order. Without relationship to a covering apostle/father (or other minister), the individual believer (or local church) is out of God's order—out from under covering and in a state of often ill-defined spiritual jeopardy.[14] In chapters 5 and 6 of this book, we examine the legitimacy of this concept in more depth. For now, our concern is the essence of what a spiritual father is.

Paul planted the church in Corinth. The Corinthians were actively rejecting him at all levels: relationally, personally, theologically, and ministerially. His response was not to assert his apostolic right, nor require their submission, nor to appeal to his office, nor require their ongoing support.[15] Rather, though loved the less for it, he was willing to spend himself, and be spent, for their sakes (2 Corinthians 12:15). His motive and actions were not to burden them, specifically financially.[16] He was concerned for them—corporately and individually—not the resources they represented to support his apostolic ministry. It is significant that the dysfunctional Corinthian church, rejecting Paul, was the place he chose to use the father-son metaphor to describe their relationship. In doing so, he was giving them the opportunity to treat him honorably *but not demanding or requiring it* as the basis of ongoing relationship. As a father, Paul was a giver, not a taker.

Now, I know the organizational relationship between a dysfunctional church and its founding apostle is not the universal standard of kingdom operations! However, the spirit, tone, and ethos that Paul manifests *is* the universal standard. He is demonstrating the qualities of genuine spiritual fatherhood.

> Behold, the third time I am ready to come to you; and I will not be burdensome to you: for I seek not yours [*finances, property, wealth*],

but you: for the children ought not to lay up for the parents, but the parents for the children.

(2 Corinthians 12:14-brackets this author's)

This fatherly apostolic quality is absent in much writing and expression in the apostolic movement as it currently stands. If we embrace the father-son metaphor of ministry, it is not the moral obligation of the children to "sustain" the fathers. That is an American, mid-twentieth-century, welfare-state entitlement spirit: "I have done my bit for you, I have put in my time, now you take care of me; you owe me." The Scriptures are so clearly opposite in tone:

Yea, ye yourselves know, that these hands have ministered unto my necessities *and to them that were with me.* I have showed you all things, how that so laboring you ought to support the weak, and to remember the words of the Lord Jesus, how he said it is more blessed to give than to receive.

(Acts 20:34-35-emphasis this author's)

Even unto this present hour we both hunger, and thirst, and are naked, and are buffeted, and have no certain dwelling place; and, *working with our own hands*: being reviled, we bless; being persecuted, we suffer it:

(1 Corinthians 4:11-12-emphasis this author's)

Paul makes it clear he worked with his own hands, likely for at least eighteen months in Corinth, and for *three years* in Ephesus to support himself, and not only himself, but through his labors, to *support others* who were with him on his team in Ephesus!

I have heard "apostolic" teaching on financial responsibility for over thirty years: not muzzling the ox, a laborer is worthy of his hire, those that preach the gospel should live by the gospel, sow sparingly—reap sparingly, sow spiritual things—reap natural things, all of which are true. The issue is not the legitimacy of these principles. It is Paul's *deference to enforce* them and his *refusal* to make them mandatory and conditional upon his involvement with people, lest the gospel suffer.[17]

In my experience I have never heard an apostle teach that not only do the "troops" have no mandatory moral obligation to support the apostle, but that the apostle should work with his hands to support the troops! If there is an obligation of support, it is not just to the apostles, but to the weak! The offering Paul was taking up in Second Corinthians 9 was not for himself, but for the poor!

I am not denying the admonitions to support ministry (apostolic and otherwise). I am asking why *no one mentions— will not even consider—* the biblical alternatives! The silence is deafening. The difference between a genuine fathering spirit and what is masquerading on the current apostolic stage is staggering.

Genuine apostolic fathers give their lives away for the children and ask nothing in return. Where a healthy atmosphere of mutuality exists, if they receive something in return, they accept it gladly and with thanks. However, true apostolic fathers do not use emotional IOUs, or spiritual manipulation on their children to psychologically extort financial support as if the children were morally obligated to do so.

In some networks and apostolic associations, the operational ethos is the exact opposite of genuine apostolic fathering. Membership in the association is sometimes contingent upon agreement and the duty of *mandatory* financial support to the overseeing apostle.[18] The plans vary from dues of some sort to a mandatory tithe of ten or sometimes twenty percent of a senior pastor's income going to the covering apostle. The issue is not presented in terms of mutuality of voluntary relationship, but as an allegedly obligatory divine order, along with the associated inferred spiritual risks and judgments should someone fail to comply with "God's standard." This is a Christian pyramid scheme.

The emphasis in these environments tends to be skewed toward the responsibilities of the subordinates to the apostolic head/father: the duties and obligations of acknowledging position, rank, loyalty, honor, authority, submission, headship, and support. The responsibility of the father to the subordinates is often ill-defined, unquantifiable, and impractical other than the alleged privilege of being under the individual's nebulous spiritual covering.

There is simply no way an overseeing apostle can functionally "father" hundreds or thousands of individuals. Even Jesus Christ limited His immediate circle to twelve! *Impartation* (preaching, teaching, inspiration, download, etc.) and spiritual blessing can occur for non-local hundreds and thousands. This is because the ability to receive impartation derives from a correct heart joining and the correct inner value systems of the individual being imparted to. The heart alignment and inner values systems allow for life transference beyond time and space.

Impartation is not defined by geographic proximity. Judas was geographically close to Jesus and heard teaching, as did all the other disciples, but he was not imparted to. Also, the age in which we live is characterized by facilitating media and communication technology we could not have dreamed of a generation ago. Even old technology can be impartational! The dead author of a book from fifty years ago can "impart" to you from beyond the grave, but he cannot father you! Impartation and relational fathering are not the same. The latter is not possible by remote signal feed. You can oversee and administrate a network from a distance, but you cannot father. It requires intimacy. Fathering takes place at an intimate and individual level rather than a corporate level; it is the dimension of mentoring.[19]

The themes of honor and submission to authority are, of course, legitimate. They are in God's Word.[20] However, they are subordinate themes. When presented in a priority and hierarchal way of obligation, rather than the mutuality found in the "one-to-anothers" of Scripture, and if void of a death and resurrection spirit, empty of love and service, they become hopelessly contaminated and betray the Spirit of Christ. It is not sound gospel ground.

When these subthemes are emphasized, a church environment can become like a spiritual plantation where the apostle is the master and production overseer of the plantation and subordinates are the slaves, not sons. The subordinates provide the resources (human, spiritual, and financial) to "fulfill the vision of the house." If after ten to fifteen years of proven "loyalty" and "sonship" and "serving another man's vision," you *may be* invited to move up from being a field slave to a house slave under the guise of opportunity for intimacy with the leader and sanctioned release into your own ministry as reward for loyalty. The problem is a change in geographic proximity does not undo a fundamentally flawed system and ethos. You are still a slave working for the master. You just get to bring him his slippers in the cool of the night instead of pick his cotton during the heat of the day.

It is one thing to spend one's self for someone. Specifics and degree of service are self-determined. It is all together another matter to be spent. That is not self-determined. It means someone else is using me up. And to experience both at a level that Paul describes as "most gladly" is beyond our reach naturally.

For example, when I go to the store and shop, I open my wallet and pay for what I want. That is spending. Going to the store, opening my wallet and saying, "Take what you want," is being spent! Genuine apostolic fathers will manifest this quality of being spent. They will give, give, give, and give again. In the face of misunderstanding, they will give. In the face of rejection, they will give. Why? Because, if genuine in fatherhood, they have touched a quality and depth of revelation of the heart of the Father that cannot help but manifest. It is their new nature to do so.

An apostolic father is not someone who requires loyalty and submission to his governmental covering as the determinative quality of his fathering status. The essence of a genuine apostolic father is one who gives his life away for those who may not appreciate it. If emphasis is on the obligations of the children to the father over the manifestation of the spirit of Christ in the fathers to the children, it is opposite of a Pauline spirit and method and is not on Calvary ground. The kingdom of God operates on relationship and mutuality, not obligation, one way or the other (more on this later). This is especially true in circumstances where intimate relationship is not functionally genuine.[21] A legitimate method with a bad spirit, or bad theology, underlying it becomes an illegitimate method. When requirement replaces love and relationship, gospel ground is lost.

I am certainly not opposed to supporting apostolic ministers and *doing so well!* Being generous is a reflection of the nature of our heavenly Father. If someone sows spiritual things, it is entirely legitimate to expect that material things would be sown back in return.[22] I am opposed to: a) codified tithe schemes of at best *dubious*, and more likely, *non-existent* exegetical base being presented as moral mandates b) the unwillingness to acknowledge other biblically-endorsed means of self-support, and c) the lack of creative financial endeavors even being considered as valid alternatives to the tithe. *Tithe schemes do not create inter-generational wealth.* They are merely *the transfer of wealth between individuals within a generation*: each generation's ministers become dependent on the current generation's tithes and offerings. There is no wealth-building future in it. Increase is only possible by adding more people: a situation begging for manipulation (conscious or otherwise). It is a maintenance model of finance. It was designed to meet the needs (maintenance) of the Levites in the Old Covenant, not as a method of generating working capital.

Jesus was spent and asked nothing for it. It was up to God the Father to decide what the Son was entitled to because of His service. In resurrection, and through the indwelling Spirit, the Son's reward is the nations.[23] A restored apostolic governmental order is not the necessary means of winning the nations. They will be won to Christ the same way as Christ received them in promise: by individual believers embracing and expressing death and resurrection life for others. This has always been, and will always be, the spirit and essence of God's governmental order.

The Old Covenant: Cinderella's Slipper

The Old Testament Scriptures frequently serve as the theological base for a good deal of teaching concerning leadership, government, and authority in the church.[24] Many view Moses, Joshua, David, Elijah, and Elisha (and others) as leadership and governmental models for the believer and the church. There is a *significant* and *fatal* flaw in this line of thinking, and the flaw produces tragic results in the church. When reading the Old Testament, the interpretive challenge is to know what to apply and what not from these stories. In terms of the inner life of a leader, there are valuable and applicable issues to learn from these stories. However, as models for systems of government and relationship between leader and those led, they are inadequate and unsuitable for the New Covenant Age. Like Cinderella's slipper and the stepsister's feet, they simply do not fit. The first-century recipients of the letter to the Hebrews did not grasp the significance of the change from the Old to the New Covenant order. It is also lost on many today. Arguing for the continuation of Old Covenant structure, Carlton Kenney says, speaking of New Testament "silence" regarding the legitimacy of a single authoritative leader in New Testament churches:

> On the other hand, if co-equality was not the way of things in the Old Testament economy, we should construe the "silence" to mean that nothing changed and *the principle is so obvious that the New Testament need not be explicit.* Indeed, if co-equality was not the way of Israel's economy, it is incumbent upon those who espouse this concept to bring forth plausible reasons for the change in the New Testament.[25]

I will accept that challenge, uh, I mean invitation. First, I would reverse the argument and say the New Testament is silent because the *change* was so *self-evidentiary* that it didn't need to be stated! The reality of Spirit-filled, kingdom-life believers were living did not need an apostolic instruction manual about who was the boss! Anyway, an argument from silence is next to meaningless, as it can be argued either way. Besides, the New Testament is not silent as Brother Kenney claims but rather quite explicit on the Old-New Covenant transition.

The Scriptures profoundly teach that when the New Covenant came into effect it was *entirely* and *qualitatively new.*[26] It is the *new* covenant. It was not *"according to"* the Old Covenant (Hebrews 8:9). This means "a *complete* and *full negation*, absolutely, intensely, objectively, deriving nothing from, downloading nothing from, or in opposition to."[27] A lack of understanding of the change in order that took place as a result of the Calvary act characterizes the church at large and the emerging authority structures in the apostolic movement.[28] It is a serious weakness in the Bible school training received by most pastors in non-denominational and apostolic churches.

I teach a course concerning the New Covenant for a Bible school. I recently taught the course in a class with four pastors of visiting churches present. In the class I have an activity where I present different propositions dealing with fundamental differences between rabbinical theology and foundational New Covenant doctrine to the class, but I do not tell them my source! (What a sneak!) I then ask the class to privately write down, as a Christian, from a Christian doctrinal perspective, whether they agree or disagree with the premises. *Without exception*, everyone in the class agreed with the premises, including the four pastors, one in particular being rather strong in his agreement. *Everywhere* I go this is the *normal* and *common* response. Uh, Houston . . . *we have a problem.* The level of saturation of Old Covenant methods, thinking, and theology *is epidemic* in the church. The gospel of grace is not well understood, and believers live and operate in a mixture of therapeutic, deistic, moral, conservatism and the Bible and think they are believers in the Lord Jesus Christ. The apostolic/prophetic movement is no exception (as evidenced by the above quote). Our ignorance shows in our theology concerning church authority structures.

Quite simply, since the day of Pentecost we are not dealing with the same kind of humanity as in the Old Covenant era. On the Day of Pentecost, for the first time in history, the divine Spirit united and resided in humanity; believing humanity became the temple of the spirit of the resurrected God-Man. John 14:17 was realized on the Day of Pentecost. At a genuine conversion, the believer literally becomes a qualitatively new creature.[29] A spirit-indwelt human simply did not exist in the Old Covenant era. A universal priesthood did not exist. A nation of priests and kings did not exist. Since the Day of Pentecost, both do. Therefore, the orders of government designed for the Old Covenant era are not suitable for the New. Philosophies, systems, mindsets, and structures derived from the Old Covenant era simply do not apply to the church. We need to limit, or at least interpret through New Covenant lenses, those leadership principles from the Old Covenant that might give us insight. Let me try a computer geek analogy. Carrying over Old Covenant principles into the New Covenant era is like trying to run Windows XP on a Windows 3.1 platform! It is all code from the same manufacturer, but your system is going to crash! The code has been upgraded! The New Covenant life is a kingdom software upgrade! It will not run on the Old code!

Some might say, "But does not the apostle teach that all Scripture is profitable for instruction and that the Old Covenant stories are there for our example?"(1 Corinthians 10:11). Indeed. I am not endorsing some Marcionite theory of negation of the Old Covenant.[30] However, the Calvary act is the great interpretive grid for the Scriptures. The interpretive question concerning the Old Covenant is not: "Is it applicable?" Rather, it is: "How is it applicable through Calvary's grid and as an example *of what?*"

When it comes to character stories, insights into human psychology, the relationship between man and God, typology, prophecy, the nature of God, etc., the Old Covenant is a legitimate source of insight.[31] When it comes to institutions, orders, and structures, the Old Covenant is not applicable. The Old Covenant stories illuminate understanding. They do not determine practice. For the New Covenant believer, the over-arching lesson gathered from the Old Testament record is: *it did not work!* In spite of all the principles, precepts, "order," structure, and teaching contained in the Old Covenant, those instructed by them, and who lived by them, were *unable* to recognize either John the Baptist or our Lord.

Here is an example of how we can gain limited insight from the Old Covenant stories but should not base our systems and structures upon them. Exodus 18:21–26 recounts the story of Moses taking Jethro's advice to delegate his leadership responsibilities, to break down management into smaller groups. Not fundamentally a bad leadership principle. Jethro exhorts Moses to pick capable, God-fearing men of truth, hating covetousness,[32] to lead and rule God's people. Aren't these great leadership qualities? Shouldn't leaders in our age be like this? Isn't Exodus 18 a "guideline" for leadership in the church? The answers to these questions are: *No, no, and no.*

In spite of all these wonderful "character qualities" and the great "principle" of delegation, how many of these principled and God-fearing individuals, hand-picked by Moses, were in a correct relationship to God in Exodus, chapters 19–20? *None.* They all missed an opportunity for a personal divine encounter at Mt. Sinai. How many of these "fine individuals" fulfilled their divine mandates and realized their inheritance? *None. They all died in the wilderness.*

The legitimate Old Covenant insight from this story is that delegation is not a bad idea. However, the Old Covenant limitation is that order, structure, character qualities, and principles *will never be enough to take a people into an inheritance!* The essentials of the New Covenant are life, relationship, and above all, faith. The quality God is looking for is faith,[33] not our moral and governmental perfections. Where He finds faith, He can bring forth moral perfections and order. He can take a faithful, weak, and disordered people who are in intimate relationship with Himself into divine destiny. But He can do nothing with non-re-lational, faithless people of impeccable character.

These things being indisputably true, why base our theology and teaching on issues of government, authority, and submission on patterns from an era and order that *failed*?! All the leadership principles displayed in the Old Testament *failed*. The people of God under their influence did not enter into spiritual inheritance. They did not find God's rest. Why carry them over? My premise is that Old Covenant leadership practices belong in the same category as Levitical priesthood practices: interesting insights, but *in application*, not appropriate for the present age. Having begun in the Spirit, are we now made perfect by the flesh? An Old Covenant map cannot lead us in the New Covenant journey.

The Man on a Throne

If we cannot look to the Old Covenant for specifics of form regarding leadership and government, is there anything the Old Covenant can teach us on the "spirit" of the subject? Yes, there is.

The book of Ezekiel opens with a heavenly vision that has been subject to endless interpretations throughout the centuries. I would like to throw my pennies into the fountain of the church's historical interpretations. I believe Ezekiel chapter one and other passages have significant insights for us on the subject of God's governmental order. There are a few key elements of the opening vision related to this subject:

- The heavenly creatures[34]
- A wheel within a wheel, full of eyes[35]
- A man on a throne[36]

I do not think it is too big a stretch to say that a vision of a man on a throne in heaven has something to do with ultimate rulership (government and order)! Likewise, I do not think it is too large a typological stretch to say that something full of eyes has to do with sight! Perhaps it would be profitable, if we want to "see" the essential qualities associated with God's government, to pay attention to this passage, in type and symbol.

The spirit of the creatures is in the wheels. The spirit of something speaks of its essence, its core, that which animates, gives life, distinguishes, identifies. Wherever the creatures went, the wheels went. The wheels were in harmonic motion with the creatures. Keil and Delitzsch say[37] that the movement was not palpable to the senses—at one level it was recognizable as movement but at another level a quality undiscernible to the natural senses. (This is an important fact for later discussion). The point is there is something more to the "movement" than the movement itself. The movement was of a spiritual quality and dimension transcending naturalistic observation and understanding. The distinguishing characteristic of the creatures and the wheels is *motion*—constant, harmonious motion. Whatever interpretation one gives this passage, one thing is clear: It is about a man on a throne and motion.

If we are going to correctly "see" issues concerning the Lord's rulership and governance, we must avoid rigid systems, interpretations, and applications of perceived "order" and embrace a fluid and imprecise understanding, annoying to natural reason. The essence of God's governmental order is Spirit-wrought and not amenable to naturalistic understanding or reduction to organizational charts. God's government is not about static placement and eternally static setting of individuals in positions and offices[38] but rather being open to the Spirit-led movements and instructions from the Man on the throne. David Cannistraci said:

> This type of flexibility within leadership of the apostles powerfully demonstrates that apostolic authority is neither *successional* (that is, able to be permanently imparted at the will of man) nor *hierarchical* (composed of numerous layers of authority) in its basic nature. Instead, leadership and submission among apostles is fluid, relational and subject to change as the situation and the will of God may dictate.[39]

At a practical local-church level, this could mean rather than having a "pastor" as the eternally-set executive office in a church, seasons might exist where one of the other ministries had a predominant function and exercise. The dominant leadership presence in a congregation needs to be flexible enough to change with stages of growth and divine seasons in a congregation. This concept's perceived impracticality has more to do with issues of financial compensation, control, and worldly management strategies than theology!

Does not this fluidity make sense from a natural parental analogy? Does not our parenting function change as a child matures? One hopes it would. Family trouble is being Fed Exed to your door if you treat an adolescent like an infant! The parental bond remains throughout the life of the child. However, the *expression* of the relationship must be open to change.

How much more so in the lives of individuals and local churches? Rigid local-church governmental structures and relationships hold individuals in eternal spiritual infancy and passivity. Spirit-wrought leadership must adapt and change to seasons of individual and congregational development. If we do our job as leaders (and people cooperate), someone who has been a Christian for fifteen years should require far less "government" than a new convert! The role, expression, and nature of the relationship of prophets and apostles within and to the local assembly are not eternally cast in theological stone.

The Scripture states that apostles and prophets are the foundational ministries of the church (Ephesians 2:20). It helps no one to continue to pour concrete once the foundation has set. The concrete will just collect in an unattractive way, making it difficult for the framers and the rest of the construction team to do their work. Paul was mobile. As a bona fide "master builder," an apostle should know the seasons of his own life. An apostle or prophet may, or may not, retain relational connections with the churches that they historically touch. However, their role and presence *must* change with time. Paul ended his ministry abandoned, alone, and in jail, not clinging to his "governmental authority" and "covering" over his network! After laying the foundation, a prophet or apostle needs to get out of the way . . . move on. . . .

CHAPTER 2

LIFE IN THREE DIMENSIONS

Obedience: God's Gift

One of the ancient heresies the early church fathers dealt with was Greek dualism. Oversimplified, dualism is a worldview that believes the universe operates under simple spiritual polarities, or dualities: good/evil, light/darkness, right/wrong, etc. A great deal of theological debate exists over how much of this kind of thought influenced the New Testament writers and how much it still influences us today. It is beyond the scope of this work to delve into the matter in detail, but it affects the discussion of authority, submission, and church government.

Unfortunately for our natural mind, God's kingdom cannot be shrink-wrapped and packaged like so much sandwich meat. It does not operate on simple dualities. One of the major changes from the Old to the New Covenant is the shift away from *quid pro quo* (Latin: "this for that") simple dualities. The Old Covenant is characterized by: do this (behave) and live (receive life as a result); fail to behave (obey) properly and you shall die (be punished, be cut off from life). If you do well, you will be blessed and if not you will be cursed.[1] The blessings and curses in Deuteronomy 28 are a classic example of the Old Covenant order of things.

Television preachers and evangelists are steeped in this utterly legal and Old Covenant mind set.[2] They have to be. Their entire system of support depends on it. Their thinking and teaching follows Deuteronomic equations like these:

God's Word + your obedience = "blessing" (usually interpreted as health, wealth, and ease)

God's Word + your disobedience = "cursing" (failure to receive the above)

Why is this message so phenomenally popular? Because the promise of reward for spiritual effort draws the spiritually still-born and blind like maggots to a corpse. It is the age-old appeal to the carnal, fallen, Adamic nature to reward itself for spiritual energy expended and spiritual pursuits attained. The obedience and reward message that saturates the airwaves effectively keeps the "seed-offerings" and "first-fruits offerings" flowing into headquarters by using God's own Word to shamelessly appeal to the believer's self-interest and keep the organization's coffers full. The New Covenant messages of forgoing our right to our own lives, His death and resurrection in us, serving Another's purposes and plan with no regard for self-interest, will empty the TV studio or the "victory living conference" faster than yelling fire in a theater.

The New Covenant reverses the Old Covenant order. It is live (receive life/blessing) and do this (behave/obey). The New Covenant equations read like this:

Receive His blessing (life) + yield to His death and resurrection = obedient fruit

You are blessed + experience His living Word = walking in obedience

We obey because obedience is consistent with our new nature, because it is right, and because the new creation is inherently empowered from within to do so.[3] Our obedience is not conditioned on the prospect of "reward." If it were so, what happens to our obedience when "blessing and reward" is slow in coming or does not arrive at all? The world is *full* of *obedient believers* who *do not experience* health, wealth, and ease. Our obedience could cost us our life, family, finances, and reputation: hardly the "guaranteed prosperity" promised on TV.[4]

If the Old Covenant is still in effect and the television evangelists are correct, what hope do you and I have of any goodness from God when our obedience is in short supply at any moment? (For myself, a frequent state of affairs!) How much obedience do we have to muster to qualify for the blessing? Is 80% obedience enough? Is 95% obedience enough? I have actually heard it said[5] that to access the "promises in His Word," only immediate, complete, 100% obedience satisfies God. Allegedly, partial or late obedience is disobedience and therefore does not qualify to receive His blessing. Since only the Son of God is perfect in His obedience, the inherently blasphemous and idolatrous thinking behind this teaching is self-evident: we become as God, and reward ourselves for it at the same time!

Thank God, that the blessing of abundant grace in the New Covenant is not dependent on my obedience to His principles, but rather my faith in Him, in me, and His death and resurrection power in me. The needed blessing of the moment is always accessible through Calvary faith, not my behavioral perfections.

In the New Covenant, God is not dependent on humanity living correctly to receive His life and blessing. He secures His own interests in humanity by putting His Spirit in us as a free gift of His sovereign and unmerited goodwill. The indwelling Spirit is both the life gift and power source. Out of the life given, behavior follows. Therefore, in the New Covenant our obedience is not our gift to God, which merits His blessing. Our obedience is His gift to us, the fruit of the life we have freely received manifested in our actions.

Now, I do not want to turn this into a theology session on the New Covenant (though God knows the church needs it), but see if this series of simple statements helps:

- Is it possible for anything from the fallen Adamic nature to satisfy God? *No!*
- Therefore, there is nothing in us, in our natural state, that desires or is able to please God. Unregenerate humanity does not love nor seek after God. *Yes*
- Therefore, in order to satisfy Himself in humanity, He must take initiation. *Yes*
- To secure His own interests, He puts His Spirit in us at conversion. *Yes*
- The new nature is now the source of our obedience to God. Where we were once unable, we are now able, due to His gift and power. *Yes*
- Therefore, since the new nature is a gift and the source of my obedience, my obedience is not my gift to God; it is God's gift to me. *Yes!*
- Therefore, I am not rewarded for my obedience because I did nothing to merit reward.[6] It is a gift. Obedience is the fruit of love. *Yes*
- Therefore, my obedience is the fruit and overflow of a life given to me, not something meritorious of blessing. It is the fruit of being blessed. *Yes*
- Therefore, in the New Covenant, I do not try to obey God and earn blessing for good behavior but live out of His life in me, which is, as Christ's own life in me, an obedient life. *Yes*

Folks, in a few sentences this is the essence of the New Covenant, and it is rarely understood.

The New Testament *quid pro quo*, if there is one, is based on life and fruit, not a businesslike transaction of "behavior and reward." A good planting, in good soil produces good fruit—it cannot help it. A tree is not "rewarded" for yielding to the life that produces from within. It produces fruit because it is in its nature to do so. In the Old Covenant (and in TV preaching) human obedience was/is the condition to receive blessing. In the New Covenant obedience is the fruit of being blessed. In the Old Covenant obedience was the root of anticipated hope. In the New Covenant, it is the fruit of realized hope. In the New Covenant, God rewards the faith filled seeker[7]—someone who maintains relationship to Himself (in strength and weakness, success and failure), not the person who most perfectly obeys His principles.

Enough Already!

The advice Job's friends gave him typifies *quid pro quo* thinking: if you do well, you prosper; if you do evil, you suffer. If you are faithful to God and follow His precepts, only blessing follows; if you don't follow His precepts, you are cursed—bad things happen to you. It is important to note that God *rebuked* Job's counselors for thinking that way. *We need to remember context.* Who was speaking to whom and in what context?

I once heard a TV preacher use a quotation from the book of Job to "prove" his extremely improper prosperity teaching along the line of: "If you live an obedient lifestyle (implying "seed offerings"), you can live in pleasure—any pleasure you want." Indeed, the verse is in the Scripture.[8] But the point the prosperity teacher failed to mention was that the source of the quote was one of Job's comforters who were all out to lunch spiritually! God rebuked Job's friends for thinking the way they did! It is almost as if after thirty chapters or so of simplistic and incorrect dualistic thinking God couldn't take it anymore and personally appears in the whirlwind to *shut them up!* Just because you can find a verse in the Bible to support your view does not necessarily mean your view is correct! Jesus in resurrection and life in the Spirit are a third alternative beyond either *quid* or *quo*! I call it third-dimension living. Let me explain.

Third-Dimension Living

Let's assume you are facing a decision. One option is choice A. That is the first dimension. The other option, perhaps the exact opposite, is option B. Typically, they are presented in an either/or fashion: this is right or wrong, good or bad. A simple diagram would look like this:

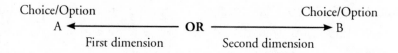

The two decisions appear mutually exclusive. This is the realm most Christians live in—struggling with issues of right or wrong behaviors. Right and wrong issues do not characterize the Spirit-led life. Death and resurrection life does. The realm of the Spirit, or the kingdom, is a third alternative, a third dimension, like this:

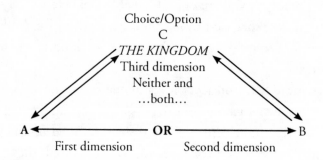

The Scriptures are full of third-dimension kingdom responses. Here are just a few examples.

In the Book of Joshua, the angel of the Lord appears, and Joshua poses a two-dimensional question: "Are you for us or against us?" The answer is "Neither, but I am come as the captain of the hosts of the Lord" (Joshua 5:14), a third-dimension response. In John 9:2, Jesus is questioned in regard to the condition of a blind man: "Who sinned, this man or his parents?" Neither. Jesus provides a third-dimension response. In John 8, the religious leaders try to capture Jesus in a two-dimensional dilemma: If He condemns the woman caught in adultery,

He has no compassion; if He releases her in mercy, He is not faithful to the Law of Moses. Jesus responds with a third-dimension kingdom reality, ignoring the polarities. In the synoptic Gospels, the Pharisees ask Jesus if it is lawful to pay taxes to Caesar: an either/or, two-dimensional polarity. Jesus responds, as always, from the heavenlies, from the Spirit, with a third-dimensional answer. One of the telltale signs of a religious spirit is forced two-dimensional polarities and an inability to touch the realm of the Spirit.

Why does third-dimensional reality relate to the matter of authority and submission and church government? Because of the tendency to define the subject and limit discussion to inadequate either/or polarities.

Those from a strong "episcopal" (ruling by the bishops/elders, etc.) governmental background will say, "Are you telling me that you don't believe in leadership and that the people should govern?" God forbid, that is the cursed rule of the Nicolaitans—the rule *of* the laity.[9] God's kingdom is not a democracy. God has given the set man the vision of the house! Anything with two heads is a monster! You can only have one executive head![10] "Crosby, you are espousing error! (or at least naiveté!)"

Those from a strong congregational, egalitarian background will say, "Do you mean to tell me that we do not have a voice? That is a formula for control and abuse of authority. Cults operate that way. We are in the New Covenant now; we are all equal. Crosby, you are espousing the dreaded rule of the Nicolaitans—the ruling *over* the laity. You are espousing error!"

As humorous as it may be, I have friends who quote the Nicolaitan verse from Revelation, each using it to condemn the other's form of government as illegitimate! The answer is neither and both. God's governmental order is a third-dimension spiritual reality. The matter can not be reduced down to simple systemic dualities such as "are we or are we not congregationally led?"

If we do not touch the Lord in third-dimensional realities, it doesn't matter a lick what form of government we practice. We are outside the realm of life and are therefore perpetrators of spiritual death, regardless of how convinced we are of the scriptural correctness our governmental order may be.

Governmental Specialists

In the Old Covenant dispensation, God's government rested on individuals specially chosen and separated for the task. The Levites were a special class. The priests were a special class. Moses, Samuel, and others were individuals separated with a unique prophetic call not available to the nation of Israel as a whole. However, Moses' dream (God's dream) was that all of God's people would be prophets (Numbers 11:29). God's Spirit in-filling of humanity on the Day of Pentecost realized this dream for Moses and God for the first time, in fulfillment of the Joel 2 prophecy. The New Covenant/Spirit age is characterized by all people, including all socially, spiritually, and culturally disenfranchised classes (women, slaves, Gentiles) being immersed in the prophetic spirit of the future age. The New Covenant era is one of universality. God's order no longer depends on a special class of anointed ministers and rulers but a nation of king-priests. What was external and unique in the Old Covenant is internal and universal in the New. This is a profound difference and distinction, and the distinction *must be maintained* when applying Old Covenant principles of authority and government in the New Covenant era.

A few specially chosen and qualified "ministers" and a lesser group of "others" do not characterize the New Covenant. Rather, the anointed individual of the Old Covenant becomes the anointed body of the New. What was on individuals in the Old Covenant (Moses, Samuel) in partiality and externality, was upon Jesus individually in fullness and indwelling, and since Pentecost, has been transferred to the body corporately in fullness and indwelling. No single believer possesses what Christ had in fullness. However, Christ was the fullness of God in bodily form, and the believing church collectively is the fullness of Christ.[11] The anointing of Christ rests on His body in a distributive sense.

Unfortunately, the King James Version inconsistently translates the Greek word *diákonos* as *minister* and sometimes *servant*. It simply means *servant*. Because the King James Version translators were in an autocratic, hierarchal, class-conscious, monarchial society, their prejudices influenced their renderings. In addition, King James VI personally pressured the translators to do the translation according to "acceptable meanings."[12] This is code-speak for: "Translate it the way I want it or you end up in the Tower with your head in your hands!" Biblically, there is no distinction between ministers and servants. It is universal servanthood—period. Just as there is universal servanthood in the New Covenant, there is universal priesthood. This is fairly well established, thanks in part to five-hundred years of Reformation teaching on the subject—for better or worse! I believe this universality has implications on our systems and orders of government.

Governmental authority is simply the right to empower and the right to limit. God's government equips and releases within the boundaries of divine calling and grace endowment[13]—empowering where *charis* (giftedness) exists and limiting where it does not. All would agree that Christ is the Executive Head of the universe and the Head of the body. As believers, we submit to His headship. The question is "*Where is Christ? How is His government yielded to in a practical way?*"

Because of inadequate understanding of the realities of the New Covenant, the Christ event, and the Spirit's indwelling, the typical response to that question is: "Christ is in heaven." If that is our perspective, the issue of authority becomes subjective and a semi-mystical submission to a remote invisible God. New Covenant reality is that Christ is no longer just in heaven but also in the believer. The temple of God is with/in humanity! Christ is in you! Christ is in me, the hope of glory! This being indisputable, what is the implication on matters of church order and church government?

It is imperative to recognize the unique deposit of Christ in each of us! Because, wherever Christ manifests, I must submit, regardless of my office, position, gender, or status in the church. I may be a water-walking apostle, but when Christ is manifest in another believer, I must submit to the incarnate Head. My position or function in the body never absolves me from submitting to Christ manifest. Being an apostle or prophet does not mean the eternal submission of others to me because of my alleged office. The governmental order of God's kingdom is defined by mutuality: "submit ye one to another in the fear of the Lord" (Ephesians 5:21). Christ administers His government by *agapē* (love) and releases it through *charisma* (giftedness). His kingdom rule is expressed through an individual's gift and calling, not positions of title and authority.

How does this work practically in a local church? Some may think my premise is hopefully naïve; that it is impossible to run a local church without a single executive head. That is likely true—within the confines of American cultural value systems of what a church is: an organization to be managed by visionary leadership that is supposed to grow to phenomenal levels of financial and numeric success. The *strong tendency* in the emergent apostolic movement to define being "apostolic" by numeric size and financial success is heartbreaking.[14] Size and money—now there are two kingdom qualities for you. The notion that size and finance are evidence of God's approving sanction is as numbingly blind as it is spiritually offensive. It is an abominable stench. The Scripture calls it mammon. It is more than the love of money. It has to do with methods and value systems. It is a spirit.

Mammon (riches) reflects the power to beautify according to the world's standards. This is not to imply that the proper use of such things [*money, material, technology*] is wrong. However, attractiveness in the sight of God has got nothing to do with them.[15]

There is nothing inherently evil with size or success unless it is used qualitatively to define size and success! By that standard, neither Jesus nor any of the first-century apostles would be included because they had neither. Perhaps if we substituted "community of faith" for "local church" and asked the same question, the proposition might not sound so naïve. It does not take much executive authority to oversee: "Love God and your neighbor as yourself."

Suppose I am a pastor and my Christ endowment lies in encouragement, care, compassion, and counseling. The sphere of my authority, the expression of Christ, should be in areas appropriate to my endowment. Simply because I am pastor does not give me divine mandate to micromanage, dictate, and control the music department, for example. I am not gifted to do it. My leadership role as equipper is to train, activate, and release others in the realm of their *charis, particularly* in areas where I, the pastor, am not endowed, even if those areas are doctrine, preaching, teaching, correction, and administration.[16]

The ungodly, unbiblical, and impossible cultural expectations put on a pastor to be and do everything are elements of the Universal Church's dysfunction. Just because we want to run the church like a New England Yankee businessman, does not mean God is obliged to bless our ethos. He won't, He doesn't, and this is why the church is broken. One's role as pastor is not to sit as executive and chief visionary but chief servant and equipper! Equipping others *is* the vision. There is no other. The role of the Ephesian 4 minister is as equipper and releaser of others into their visions, not getting his/her own vision and making others submit to it.

Much of the visionary language used in leadership schools draws upon American cultural models, the lure of success, and Old Covenant theologies, rather than New Covenant revelation. Being the "visionary" sounds good, seems legitimate, but in practical application, always ends up abusing and hurting people because it is not based in God, His Word, or His Spirit in accuracy (see chapter 7). God's government rests within the sphere of grace endowment and no further. It is not positionally defined; it is functionally limited.

A Little Leaven

Leaven in Scripture represents both positive and negative spiritual qualities. Positively, leaven represents kingdom influence; negatively, sin. I have often wondered why for a Semitic[17] mind leaven would be used metaphorically for these qualities. A little cultural background is helpful.

A Semite's worldview of commerce, the universe, and resources was finite.[18] The concept of wealth generation through capital investment as increasing total available resources simply was not in their worldview. To them, the world was finite. If you get a bigger piece of the pie, it means someone else gets a smaller part, and the cosmic balance is upset. Therefore, knowing one's "place" in the greater scheme of things, and staying there, was very important.

Boundaries of all sorts—social, spiritual, cultural—were very important. Gender, class, and religious boundaries characterized not only Old Covenant theology and practice but deeply influenced the Semitic mind. For example, if you were the son of a fisherman, it was your God-ordained destiny to be one also. It was your boundary, your limitation. Attempting to improve your lot, to move up the ladder from fisherman to architect (self-initiative that we in the West would greatly admire), would not have been admired but rather considered "uppity"[19] and inappropriate because it is an attempt to exceed divinely-ordained boundaries.

What has this got to do with leaven? Leaven is a substance, which, by its nature refuses to stay contained. It always exceeds its boundaries. This is why it came to be viewed metaphorically for sin. For a Semite, it was sinful to go beyond one's boundaries. On the positive side, the irrepressible expansion of the kingdom of God is likened to leaven because it is in its nature to expand. It can not be stopped.

Now, we do not import first-century culture into our era, but we can make an application.

Tragedy in the church results when believers and leaders fail to recognize and attempt to operate outside the limitations of their Christ endowment. Exercising executive leadership authority outside of one's Christ endowment, from a "position or office" rather than function and endowment, *invariably* results in disorder, relational disintegration, and personal pain on both sides of the pulpit rather than the hoped-for order that releases blessing. The Holy Spirit is obliged to anoint only that which He endows. He is not obliged to anoint our Western, organizational, success-and-growth-oriented methodologies that are so easily energized by the Adamic nature as a counterfeit church.

The Myth of the Servant Leader

If ink were water, commentary on the servant leader would fill the Sea of Galilee. It is the near-universal standard ascribed to the ideal church leader. It is one of the church's biggest myths. The ancient Greek and Roman gods of mythology were not deities, as we understand the term. They were magnified humans: comprehensible in similarity to reality but enlarged into fantasy. The servant leader is the Sasquatch of the kingdom: folks claim to have seen one, but a confirmed capture is elusive. In my personal local church experience, I know a lot of people who *think* themselves servant leaders and who *talk* about servant-leading, but I have never seen one—including myself. Believing in Peter Pan is relatively harmless. Believing I can fly, and acting out of my belief, will yield a high-speed appointment with the pavement. So it is with the archetype servant leader. It is legitimate in theory but fantasy in implementation. Building life around a fantasy does not produce God's desired result. It produces pain.

The words, *servant* and *leader*, are so loaded with cultural preconceptions, it is nearly impossible to extract a scriptural definition of either.[20] Technically, it is not a biblical expression. Rather, it is a linguistic vise allowing us to rationally hold and process two antinomic qualities in Christ. We culturally define these words in terms of role, function, and character qualities: a servant is subservient, a leader assertive. A slave (*doulos*) serves; a ruler rules. How obviously self-evident! Not necessarily.

Some ministers emphasize the leader side of this antinomy: I am the leader, I get the vision, I get the direction, I get the call, I get the dream, you all fall into line, you must submit, don't dare get out of governmental alignment (code words for: I control everything, but I am really serving you).

Some churches and saints emphasize the servant element of the antinomy: "Pastor, we don't care about your vision. We want you to care for us. You are supposed to lay down your life for us, putting our needs before your own. Your calling is to be the chief servant. You need to back off all this 'leadership talk' and take a towel and wipe our feet. My sick aunt needs you to visit her now, and you need to be at my cousin's birthday party this weekend, and the church sidewalk needs to be shoveled, and since you are drawing a salary we think you need to do this before Thursday, because, after all, your call is as the servant of all."

The corrupt distortion of the servant expectation makes the pastor little more than an errand boy sent by God to meet the needs of the flock. Once, in a meeting with pastors in a community where I lived, I heard a pastor from a fundamental evangelical church say that he was exhausted, overworked, and abused. However, he also said this was fine because that is what the servant of all is supposed to experience; like lambs led to the slaughter, we are not to lift our voice. The pastor thought he was modeling the servant leader. He was, of course, doing nothing of the sort. This pastor's paradigm of ministry was not biblical servanthood. It was abuse masquerading in a religious spirit.

Mix the idyllic servant-leader myth with unsanctified character traits or personality quirks and deficiencies and either extreme—strong set-man leadership or high-shepherd's touch servanthood—becomes abusive: authoritarianism on the one hand and enablement and codependency on the other.

These terms must be stripped of first-century cultural biases and protected from twenty-first century cultural incursions. The Christ Event[21] forever elevated these terms to a kingdom dimension. For the believer, the outpoured and indwelling Spirit makes both terms *equalizing qualities of empowerment*, not limiting roles or functions.[22] *In the kingdom, servants lead and leaders serve.* Slaves rule[23] and rulers labor.[24]

From a biblical perspective, the phrase, "servant leader," is a meaningless tautology.

The Christian community expects the ideal Christian leader to model both qualities to the fullest degree possible, thus reflecting the image of Christ (as all *good* Christians should, *especially* those called to lead). I doubt if any scholar, teacher, or practical minister seriously thinks any one individual embodies the fullness of Christ's gifts or character qualities. Why is it then assumed that the fullness of the idyllic servant leader should manifest in every leader? Could partiality or lack in either element be acceptable or even divine purpose?

Garçon, Service Please!

I have yet to meet a church leader who, when asked, didn't think him or herself a decent servant leader, at least trying to emulate Christ in ministry.[25] Frank self-assessment is undoubtedly a healthy practice. Submission to superiors is commendable. These alone, however, are insufficient. It is like a surgeon whose patients all die. A pat on the back from the boss for an artful suture on a dead patient does not testify well to a surgeon's skill. An incompetent waiter does not get to tell the customer the tip amount. *The recipient of the service*[26] determines its value. Those *served*, not the *server*, evaluate the quality of servant-leading!

For many years, I worked in metallurgical and process engineering for Corning, Inc. in Corning, NY. Two of the most progressive features of Corning's human-relations policies were:

1. Subordinates participated in the interview process of potential candidates for jobs superior to their own.
2. Subordinates participated in the performance review process of their own boss or superior.

In terms of candor and minimized office politics, it was the most enjoyable work atmosphere I have experienced. The climate was one of mutuality: critique and evaluation went upstream, not just downstream.

Mutuality is a quality sorely lacking in many authority and submission structures in the church. Too often honor and deference flow upstream toward position, title, and giftedness rather than to the least comely member.[27] The children of this age are wiser than the children of light.[28]

Among independent and nondenominational churches with an episcopal form of government,[29] few leaders are open to objective, third-party assessment of skill and ability. Some are accountable in matters of doctrine and morals to peers or superiors (behavioral accountability). However, in my personal sphere of influence I know of only a handful open to systematic and regular skill evaluation and development—from anyone—peer or otherwise. Insecurity in ministers knows no bounds.

The notion of submitting to the opinions of subordinates is *viscerally repugnant* to the set-man style of leadership:[30] "What? Ask the people what they think? Let them measure us? Why, the next thing you know we will be laity-led (you guessed it), the curse of the Nicolaitans! Congregationalism! Democracy! Man's system in the church! The rule of the people! We go to the mountain. We are the Moses' of the New Covenant. We get God's word, vision, and direction and present it to the people to follow. We have the call to lead! The people need to covenantally trust us and submit. Shepherds lead, sheep follow! That's God's order! Don't come out from under God's covering! God uses the sheep metaphor for a reason. Sheep are stupid! They will over graze if left to themselves. God calls you sheep; therefore, you need to submit and follow us."

Talk about overdoing a metaphor! I wish I were joking. I wish I were making up every one of the preceding clauses. Unfortunately, I have heard *every one of these*, their variants and more, preached with dogmatic fervor during my experience across a broad spectrum of Christianity.

God forbid that we, as leaders, should actually consider the feelings of those we are leading! The strong set-man style of leadership, energized by Old Covenant leadership theology, is inherently not conducive to evaluation, *especially from subordinates*. Insecurities and personality issues just exacerbate the problem. I am not saying that evaluation from the congregation is necessarily *determinative* on any matter, it is *contributive*: valued, sought after, honored, highly weighted, given serious consideration. Remember, in the New Covenant, every believer has the Spirit of God, not just Moses and a few specially anointed individuals as in the Old Covenant. Most set-men type leaders don't even believe in contribution from the rank and file. They are locked in an Old Covenant leadership model that elevates them as "constitutionally different" than those they lead. They would deny it in doctrine, but it is a reality in practice. Peers, elders, and friends allegedly hold them accountable. This accountability is only legitimate if the peers, elders, and friends have the right to tell the set man no; they must have the authority to deny him and fire him. If that dynamic is not present, it is just a common dress monarchy without scepter robe and crown.

I do not deny the need for the more disciplinary or "strong" elements of leadership from time to time. Nor am I endorsing taking the eternal pulse of people in order to make leadership decisions. A general may have authority over his troops by reason of experience and rank. However, if he does not have the heart of his troops, he will lead an army of one—himself. One day, in the heat of battle, he just might find a bullet in the back of the head. If a set man's vocabulary[31] is predominantly saturated with the language of honor, government, authority, and submission rather than love, care, and service, there may be a laser scope pointed in his direction. A wise leader will make sure the troops are with him, not just his adjutant staff!

Biblical Idealism

It might be argued that realization of the ideal servant leader is possible with God: what is impossible with man is possible with God. If we just did things right enough, we would be in God's order, the Holy Spirit accomplishing what we cannot if we would just carefully align with the precepts in God's Word. I would respond that we are the church on earth, not in paradise. While we hold to, and progress toward, an ideal, we live in reality. Sticking our heads in the sand of biblical idealism while ignoring natural dynamics of interpersonal human relationships is a curse in the church. At times we cannot see past idyllic biblicism to the level of everyday human interactions. Throw in reactionary fundamentalist tendencies against anything remotely psychological as "humanism from the devil," and it is a wonder the church functions *at all*. Well, it often doesn't.

The instant two human beings are in the same room trying to get along, there will be some manifestation of leader and follower. If not, they will either separate or kill each other! It is a function of human dynamics, not church meeting structure and form. Those wounded from authority figures often retreat into reactionary meeting structures attempting to avoid leadership abuse: all are supposedly equal, no one possessing directive authority.

There is a legitimate place for the authoritative teaching of the Word. Without it, we will be left with egalitarian subjectivism, and the church will become a mere focus group of shared opinions. This is a real danger in the nontraditional house churches that are emerging across the world. The response to abusive leadership is not "non-leadership." It is recovery of a New Covenant, Calvary platform of leadership free of legalism, Old Covenant theology and methods, and self-serving personal agenda.

We can dispense with name, position, and title, but the human dynamic will remain. *Someone*—by gift mix, age, temperament, skill, experience, resources, or personality—*will* emerge as the *de facto* leader. Retreat into a form of spiritual egalitarianism or recovering some allegedly divinely proscribed meeting structure from the book of Acts does not negate the reality. The matter is divinely programmed into humanity. We can run from it, suppress it, bury it, chain it, deny it, rail against it, curse it, judge it, dodge it; someone will lead, somehow, some way. The issue for the believer is keeping leadership on a New Covenant footing: death and resurrection, Spirit indwelling, charismatic endowment and function.

Nobody's Got it All

Some leaders are very good executives in a Western, hierarchal, administrative, corporate sort of way. Others excel in service in a Western, managerial, busyness, efficient, vocational, "ministerial" sort of way. There are often temperament, calling, and gift mixes with elements of both. However, a kingdom, death/resurrection-based, Christ-form of biblical leadership embodied in a single individual is as rare as ham salad at a bar mitzvah. I am not sure it is legitimate to expect otherwise.

Visionary leaders are said to serve the body with their "visionariness." (See chapter 7 for a biblical definition of what it actually means to be a visionary leader, for now, I will let it stand as it is normally understood.) While perhaps technically true at a ministerial level, it is not true at a practical and interpersonal level. The candid reality is most visionary leaders are not good practical servants and often weak at an interpersonal level. It is grossly unfair to project a high-servant quotient upon a visionary leader—believing he or she is deficient because of a perceived lack of servanthood or "a warm personal touch." Unrealistic expectations fuel relational breakdown. Visionary leaders may experience psychological, relational, and religious pressure to be more servant-like, neutralizing their visionary grace.

On the flip side, projecting visionary expectations on a practical, high-touch, highly empathetic, caretaking, shepherd/leader is likewise unfair.[32] Because of the high touch leader's lack of visionary thrust (and often accompanying poor administrative and formal communication skills), subordinates often assume directive initiatives, inappropriately crossing lines of charismatic boundary endowment. Illegitimate expectations upon a high-servant quotient leader produce an abiding sense of failure, comparison, discouragement, lack of acceptance, and restless striving likewise neutralizing his or her grace. This all results from the mythology of the idyllic servant leader. Consider the statistics from *Beyond all Limits* by Bill Bright and James Davies:[33]

- Each month fifteen hundred pastors leave the ministry due to moral failure, spiritual burnout, or contention in their church.
- Ninety percent said the ministry was completely different than they thought it would be when they entered ministry.
- Eighty percent of pastors and eighty-four percent of their spouses feel unqualified and discouraged in their role in ministry.
- Eighty percent of seminary and Bible school graduates who enter the ministry will leave it within the first five years.
- Ninety percent of pastors said their seminary or Bible school training did only a fair to poor job of preparing them for ministry.
- Fifty percent are so discouraged that they would leave the ministry if they could, but have no other way to make a living.
- Seventy percent of pastors do not have a close friend, confidant, or mentor.
- Eighty percent of pastors surveyed spend less than fifteen minutes a day in prayer. Ninety-five percent do not regularly pray with their spouse.
- Seventy percent of pastors said the only time they spend studying the Word is when they are preparing sermons.
- Eighty percent of pastors' spouses feel their spouse is overworked.
- Almost forty percent polled said they had an extramarital affair since beginning their ministry.
- Fifty percent of pastors' marriages will end in divorce.
- Eighty percent of adult children of pastors surveyed have had to seek professional help for depression.

There is no shortage of pain on both sides of the pew. What will it take for us to admit that our concepts, methods, and philosophies of church government and ministry are broken and need to be reconfigured from top to bottom? Why is it so common in the church that dysfunctionality is clung to so strongly in the name of defending truth?

Make Sure the Shoe Fits

Perpetuating the archetype servant-leader myth in the church causes untold sorrow in the lives of ministers and congregations. A congregation's (traditional, house church, cell) expectations in their leadership must match that leader's grace. If a congregation expects a dominant visionary leader but receives a servant, or if it expects a dominant servant ministry and gets a visionary one, it will experience confusion, hurt, and relational disintegration that may never be recoverable. Ministers, unwanted and unloved, feel stuck in a hellish assignment. Congregations, misunderstood and hurt, change pastors like a pair of socks.

The servant-leader siren song destroys good people on the rocks of psychological projections and religious expectations. Like someone caught in a dead-end alley and about to be mugged, frantic survival instincts kick in over reason and mutual understanding.

Conclusion

If there is any lesson to be had from the New Covenant, particularly the book of Acts and the Epistles regarding patterns and order, it is that in the post-Pentecost Spirit age *there is no pattern*! Christ in resurrection is the Pattern! Our pattern is a person not a plan. There is no pattern method of healing. There is no pattern method of ministry. There is no pattern method of church form. There is no pattern of government and authority structures.

The New Testament pattern is to see the Man on the throne in resurrection, through the revelation of His Word by the Spirit, and do what He says! The Word is broad enough to encompass diversity and flexibility. It has been divinely left vague on these matters of government because the Holy Spirit knows man's propensity to codify everything into systems of order. If God is calling you to build a mega church, build it! Full steam ahead, captain! May your seas be calm and your sails full! If He is calling you to operate a home church, do it! Just don't worship at the shrine of the non-leader who leads! The era we live in is characterized by death, resurrection, love, service, and liberty; not government, order, authority, and structure.

> We are not called to find the right pattern and then implement it. We must respond to him who is the head of the church and submit to his initiatives as He implements his will among us.[34]

CHAPTER 3

I HAVE IT ON
HIGHER AUTHORITY?

Be a good citizen. All governments are under God. Insofar as there is peace and order, it's God's order. So live responsibly as a citizen.[1]

Let every soul be subject unto the higher powers. For there is no power but of God: the powers that be are ordained of God.[2]

Of the increase of His government and peace, there shall be no end.[3]

In Romans 13:1–2, Paul admonishes the Christians in Rome to obey their civil authorities. He refers to "higher powers" (Gr. *huperexoúsais*, superior authority) as a group or class. In its most literal sense, the word/prefix translated as *higher* means "superior in rank." We must be very careful applying this verse. It contextually speaks of *civic authority*. What might suitably describe civic authority structure may or may not be applicable to authority structure in the kingdom. One thing is certain. *Any* application of this verse that imposes cultural presuppositions or biases is illegitimate. In American culture, higher authority invariably conjures vertical, top-down, boss-and-subordinate ideas in our minds.

Jesus clearly said that the ethics of vertical layer hierarchy should *not apply* to His followers.[4]

This being true, the idea of levels of authority seems well attested by other Scripture in both Testaments:

- Ephesians 6 speaks of principalities, powers, and rulers, at least inferentially indicating rank in the spirit realm.
- The biblical concept of archangel (Gr. *archon, ruler*) as compared to lower classes of angels and cherubim points toward rank among the angels.
- In the Old Testament there were priests, Levites, and the high priest. Each a different class of rank.
- Moses set established leaders in Israel based on tiers or rank: leaders of tens, fifties, hundreds, etc. (Exodus 18).
- Jesus differentiated the seventy from the multitudes, the twelve from the seventy, and Peter, James, and John from the twelve (Luke 6; Matthew 17; Luke 10).
- While we want to be careful in reading too much into a metaphor in a single verse, it appears there may have been some rank among the apostles (Galatians 2:9).

What then does "higher authority" look like in a kingdom model? What exactly does it mean to be subject to them? The answer to this question is essential as remediation for abuse at either end of the authority spectrum.[5] Authority, exercised from position rather than Calvary/covenant love is control. It takes more than token lip service to "servant leadership" to genuinely manifest legitimate authority. The church is maintained by three essentials: life, liberty, and authority. The indwelling Spirit enables us to obey. Love without authority or discipline is license for anarchy. However, unrestrained human psychological sensitivities do not constitute biblical love. Authority is the empowering arm muscle that calls love into acts of service for the increase of the body and the care of the world. Love is the water that runs within the banks of discipline and order. Either alone is unacceptable.

Below are eight distinct levels of authority (perhaps there are more) in God's kingdom listed by rank. They are not equal. Each believer needs to learn what it means to be subject to the "higher authorities" lest we succumb to false honor and obeisance to church leaders or the other extreme of subjective independence. Walking in the revelation of the Calvary Spirit is the only way to safely navigate these extremes.

The authority we are most familiar with in the church is primarily "positional authority." I refer to it as delegated authority. This authority is exercised by leaders, pastors, etc. It is the second from the bottom in rank and importance. I think this is significant. The "higher authorities" are:

1. sovereign, imperial authority of the Lord in His person
2. authority of His Word
3. legal authority
4. authority of conscience
5. authority of family
6. functional authority
7. delegated authority
8. authority of custom

Sovereign Authority

Sovereign authority rests in the person of Christ. It is His imperial, individual, kingly, personal authority over the cosmos and all that is in it. His sovereign authority is the right Christ possesses as Judge of the living and the dead, King of kings, and Lord of lords. It is the fruit of His willingness to taste death and resurrection for us.[6] He is the ultimate authority in every believer's life to whom all will give answer.

No man, church, organization, leader, mentor, discipler, spiritual father, pastor, wonder worker, apostle, nor prophet has the right to usurp this authority in an individual believer's life, nor come between the believer and the Lord in some misguided semi-mediatory concept of spiritual covering and mentoring. For better or worse, each believer is ultimately responsible directly to the sovereign King. Too often, God's leaders, as undershepherds, transgress this authority in believers' lives under a misguided sense of what it means to teach or disciple others, especially in circles where "accountability" is emphasized. The believer belongs to Him, not us. There is only one Judge and His Word. He is the living Lord over His Book and flock. A leader is, at best, a steward of another man's inheritance. The sheep belong to Him. They are kept by His saving grace, mediated by the person of the Holy Spirit, not as a result of our brilliant, cutting-edge, and revelatory preaching!

The Authority of the Word

Not far below Christ's sovereign authority is the authority of His Word. God is the Word and the Word is God. The Holy Spirit inspired the Word. He is the Spirit of Truth. Christ is the incarnate Logos. The Scriptures are literally the expression of His person. When illumined by the active work of the Spirit, they are just as alive as is His person and require the same submission. The intellectual understanding and application of His Word has neither life nor authority. In charismatic circles, subjective impressions are often elevated and taught as more than things personally edifying but as instruments of instruction for others to conform to or live by. This is heresy.

No subjective dream, vision, prophecy, insight, etc. is of the same stature of the revealed will of God in the Scriptures. It is there that we should place our emphasis, not on subjective feelings and impressions. God *already has spoken in, through, and by the Son* (Hebrews 1:2), literally, in a "sonly" way. He, the Son, *is* the more sure word of prophecy.[7] His person and His written Word deserve responsive obedience. The novel musings of what may or may not pop into an apostle or prophet's head deserve scrutiny and evaluation, not obedience. Subjective musings may be edifying, but they are not binding in any dimension.

After thirty years in the church (half of it in formal ministry), I am convinced that, in spite of all our teaching efforts, the overall biblical literacy of the average American Christian is woefully low. Some of Mr. Barna's statistics indicate this is this case. The little the saints do seem to possess tends to have no worldview mooring[8] and to be very "proof-texty." After getting past the threshold of a few chain-linked memorized verses, for many, there is nobody home. Unhealthy dependency on pulpit ministry promotes passivity in the hearer. Our job as leaders is to equip others to handle the Word of God accurately for themselves, not keep them dependent on our exegetical and pulpit abilities. Failure here opens the door to unhealthy co-dependencies and control. Insecure leaders and lazy saints, frankly, are content with the arrangement.[9]

The leader's role is to work him or herself out of a job. We begin by interpreting the Word to new converts until we equip them with the tools to do it themselves. Then we need to get out of the way! So much Sunday morning activity is nothing more than the carnal thrill a pulpit minister gets from having a regularly captive audience in awe of his great revelation and oratorical skills. The spoon-fed congregation comes to be impressed by the latest cutting-edge revelation rather than being practically equipped to handle the Word of God themselves.

The highest function of the prophetic ministry is not to broker divine thought and understanding to others. The highest prophetic function is not telling others what you see. It is the ability to give (impart) to others the faculty of divine sight![10] Our call as leaders is to put the believer and the Lord into a hand-to-hand and face-to-face relationship, not keep them lapping at the trough of our biblical insights. If we are standing by, trying to arrange the fingers in the divine handshake, we are meddlesome controllers, transgressing this second tier of authority. Our authority as leaders does not extend to the eternal brokering of the Word of God to the believer.

First-generation, resurrection-witnessing, dead-raising, miracle-working apostles taught the Bereans, and they were commended for checking things out! If the first-century saints are thus commended, how much more should we, two thousand years later, do likewise? For some reason, professional ministry attracts insecure people like bees to honey. They mistakenly expect personal validation through the acclaim that can accompany pulpit ministry—the perceived admiration of others. However, their personal insecurity is threatened when instead of doe-eyed awe and admiration they are met with honest inquiry, examination, and questions presented in a right spirit.[11]

When emphasis on honoring leadership (and it frequently is over-emphasized) combines with a celebrity spirit that accompanies any form of success in an American paradigm, leaders begin to believe their own press reports about how wonderful they are. A subtle spirit of "immunity" creeps in. Woe to the leader who dismisses every honest inquiry as either beneath his dignity to address or who attributes it to disloyal, dishonoring, rebellious, deceived saints who just need to submit. Leaders owe it to God's flock to fully equip them to handle the Word accurately for themselves and to honestly answer *any* question given in a right spirit. Insecure leaders are intimidated by inquiring minds larger than their own. Inquiry is not subversion.

Legal (Contractual) Authority

This level of authority is the level of civic affairs, legal matters, contracts, etc. Paul was not one to flout civil authority. Nor was Jesus, as demonstrated in the famous "render unto Caesar passage."[12] Paul's handling (or non-handling!) of the slavery issue displays his sensitivity to prevailing legal authority as well as cultural authority. Contrary to some popular images in the quasi-religious or secular media, neither Jesus nor Paul were populist anarchists. They were not there to overturn social orders. They preached a kingdom that transcended the social structures of the time and still does.

As believers we are obliged to submit to those legal contracts, compacts, decrees, and laws that are enacted by civil and legal authorities. Our status in the kingdom does not make us immune from the laws of the land. I have known too many Christians who use their faith to cheat (such as working under the table for cash), because they feel they are above complying with the "illegitimate" laws of the land. In a representative republic, we get the laws we deserve. We cannot appeal to the authority of conscience in the presence of injustice. There would be no end to that. If injustice prevails, it is because we have facilitated it. Corruption requires flow: benefactor and beneficiary. Institutional corruption is just self-interest magnified into a corporate expression in the fabric of a society. Short of causing us to deny our faith or curse God, the believer is to comply with civil authorities,[13] and, if he or she must, because of deep conviction on a moral issue, live with the consequences and comfort of being morally right and legally wrong.

Authority of Conscience

Whatsoever is not of faith is sin. (Romans 14:23)
. . . their conscience bearing them witness. (Romans 2:15)

This is a bit tricky. I debated where to place the authority of conscience, before or after legal authority. Within the arena of the church, I believe the placement is correct. Conscience is higher than the realms in the following sections. However, engaged in the civic arena, civil law supersedes conscience, unless it is a Daniel-type situation where our faith in God is being directly assaulted—then conscience rules. There is no basis for Christians to cavalierly flout civic authority.

There are many areas of life in which the Scriptures are silent, vague, unclear, or in tension. In those areas, our conscience is the higher authority to which we must yield. The authority of conscience is higher than pastoral or apostolic opinions in these matters. For example, some areas where the authority of conscience might apply in a local church setting are

- types and styles of music
- to wear makeup or not

- dating
- TV
- movies
- hair styles
- ethics in raising children
- clothing style
- toys—"holy ones and non-holy ones?"
- church membership
- Sunday school
- the arts

New Covenant Scripture is not explicit on these themes. We must preach and require what is sure, core, and clear; not the marginal issues of life that change, ebb, and flow with the passing of time and culture. It is a mistake to preach personal preference and conviction as binding doctrine. Unfortunately, it happens all the time.

The Westminster Confession of Faith is, as a whole, a very well thought out document of the church. In it, the Westminster divines succinctly address the issue of silence of Scripture and our interactions as believers and leaders. They wrote the following as self-evident truth:

- Nothing contrary to Scripture can ever be true.
- Nothing in addition to Scripture can ever be binding; it may be true.
- In essentials, conformity; in non-essentials liberty; and in all things charity (love and kindness).

Now, others may advise and entreat us and perhaps provide helpful wisdom and insight on unclear or marginal issues. But they may not legitimately exercise rank and position to enforce conformity in areas where conscience is the higher authority. God's leaders regularly violate the authority of conscience in the lives of those under their charge. Topical preachers whose emphasis is on "things" and "isms," "themes and trends"[14] rather than Christ and Him crucified are particularly vulnerable to violate another's conscience because they cannot allow others freedom in marginal areas. Today's secular fad becomes the obsessive topic of "touch not the unclean thing" preaching. Likewise, overly compassionate leaders, who are more enablers than nurturers, frequently will not yield to the authority of conscience, as they are afraid an individual may make a wrong decision and somehow be hurt.

If an overly sentimental spirit gets a hold of discipleship, it will turn into the eternal nursery of fear and control. Spiritual growth does not happen in the warm womb of maternal paranoia. It happens on the dangerous edge of real life. If you want your children to learn to ride a bicycle, you must take the training wheels off sooner or later. They *will* fall over. They *will* get hurt. I have learned that my education and spiritual growth occurs the most through what I do wrong, not what I do right. Inordinate concern over believers making a mistake is not mentoring or biblical discipleship.

The Scriptures do not tell you who to marry, what job to take, where to move, etc. We can get advice and counsel in these situations in life, but no apostle or minister has the right to tell you what you should do and demand compliance with his decree, nor treat you as rebellious if you do not follow the advice. To do so violates the authority of conscience. If individuals reject your counsel and advice, so be it. Do not insist on others listening to you. If they err, they err.

Often an individual's actions based on conscience will be wrong, lead them to a mistake or even personal pain. This does not give the apostle or minister the right to enforce his perceptions nor play "I-told you-so" games. The nature of growth in a free atmosphere of the Spirit is the freedom to be wrong. We are not free to sin. But we must be free to make big mistakes. We must speak boldly and directly concerning paths that are explicitly sin, but in gray areas, or where the issue is a "cultural conviction" rather than an explicit biblical one, we must not require conformity or withdraw from the community because of a lack of perceived compliance. The more God entrusts to us personally, the more liberty we are likely to grant others. Freedom requires risk.

There is no single area that Christians routinely violate more than the authority of conscience. When we think it is our business to get others to conform to what we think is important, we are not of God's Spirit, but rather, a spirit of coercion, a crusading spirit not unlike militant Islam. We do not kill with bomb and gun, but with our tongue in slander and gossip, separating from one another based on what we think is righteous. Often what appears on the surface as a commitment to biblicity on an issue, a commitment to a standard, is really about power, authority, and control. If we examine others in such a scrutinizing way, who examines us in like fashion?

There may be many paths of wisdom and prudence to which the Scriptures say nothing. Everything may be lawful, but not all things are profitable.[15] It is in these areas that the law of liberty and the authority of conscience prevails. In it, we have the right to be wrong, mistaken, and even stupid. It is the price of liberty. Making others come to our point of view on marginal issues is not our calling. Our call is to lay down our lives for one another, not coerce each other into ideological and behavioral conformity.

Authority of Family

God established the family as an institution before the church, its offices, and ordinances. The family is the smallest church unit, and how badly things are broken in this regard in our culture needs no amplification! Church may not override family authority. The two realms, family and church, though integrated, must remain separate. The church and its leaders have no authority to tell you how to run your family except in those matters that are explicitly sin. The church has authority to demand and require that sin cease. However, there are many other areas of life that are less than optimal that are not overt sin. Church leaders can entreat, implore, offer wisdom and advice, but they may not demand compliance.

Routine violation of the authority of family occurred in three different church scenarios with which I am personally acquainted.[16] In these environments, the church authority structure got so out of hand that the leaders told people who they could or could not marry and what job they could take. Parents often played no role in these decisions in the case of minors or young adults. To have the local leadership "bless" or "sanction" a marriage, the individuals had to appear before a "court," or tribunal, of hand-picked elders and get permission from the court to marry or not marry an individual. Church leadership often disallowed parents from being on the review court as not being spiritual enough to make sound judgments. The rationale for this behavior was "courtship instead of dating," "being submitted," "staying under covering," "keeping covenant," etc. This is, of course, legal, cultic abuse. However, the fundamental problem is recognizing appropriate lines of authority. Conscience and family are higher authorities than ministry office and calling.

On the converse side of things, families do not have the right to rule the church. You may not project personal family values for your children on the church as a whole and expect the church to come around to seeing it your way. As an example, I have seen circumstances where a particular family will develop a "conviction" that they don't want their sons playing with toy guns because it allegedly promotes violence and aggression. While I don't agree with that, a family is certainly within its rights to raise its children with that value system. However, that family does not have the right to march into a leader's office and demand the church take a stand for righteousness on that issue, demanding corporate conformity to their conviction. The family may, if they so desire, not participate in events or activities in which they deem their family convictions compromised. They are not justified in socially or psychologically marginalizing other families who do not share the conviction.

Unfortunately, in the American church experience, the family with the conviction will likely leave and attend a church that agrees with them on the marginal conviction and thus endless church fragmentations and the spawning of myriad sects whose rallying and unifying center is no longer Christ and Him crucified.

Your authority of family does not outrank the other's authority of conscience.

Functional Authority

Too often our church motto seems to be, "I may not know what I am doing, but bless God, I am in charge!" We structure our organizations around those who are faithful and loyal, not necessarily the best equipped. A simple lack of human resources frequently forces small churches to this place: "Please . . . help us . . . any warm and willing body will do!"

Authority is based on ministry, and ministry is based on death and resurrection. There is no ministry without authority and no authority without death and resurrection. When authority exceeds ministry, it is positional and has no spiritual substance. Functional authority originates in the area of my expertise. It is the place of effective service, activated by the Spirit.

Three areas serve as the source of individual functional authority: 1) birth (natural talents: general grace given to all humanity), 2) training, and 3) supernatural gifting. Within the church, there is often unnecessary reaction to the first two. Common grace has touched all humanity in the Creation. Even if we are not serving God, we are gifted and talented at birth. Second, authority comes from skills we gain through education and life experience. Functional authority comes from serving others not just in the area of natural giftedness or talent, but also through those gifts that are charismatic endowments or Spirit—energizings—part of the grace package we receive at conversion. It is so critical to recognize each of these three graces.

From a local church perspective, God occasionally administers His grace to us directly, but usually it comes through another body member.

God designed functional authority in another member to replenish or fill our own lack. We miss functional authority at our own peril. Missing it causes us to associate people with tasks, or demand of them services, for which they are not suited, simply because they are faithful and available! Don't ask the accountant to do the inner healing ministry team (unless supernaturally endowed). Don't ask a prophet to be the door greeter! We need to pay attention to people and equip and release them into areas of functional authority for which they are suited! We need to teach others to submit when in the arena of another's functional authority!

The concept of functional authority can be hard to grasp because of our long-standing traditions of positional and hierarchical authority structures. Let's take a look at several examples of how functional authority might work.

You are in a tragic car accident. Your arm is lying ten feet away from where it should be, and there is blood everywhere. Three people are bystanders: a person who by birth is very caring, a Hindu female doctor, and an apostle/prophet from your network or association with the gift of discerning of spirits. If you were the victim in the accident, whom would you want giving immediate instructions in that situation? The prophet? Because he is a Christian and can "discern" (supposedly) the angel of death over you? The apostle? Because men are supposed to have "authority" and be in charge? How absurd. Of course you would want the doctor (regardless of gender, religion, or rank) in charge and making decisions because she has *functional authority* in that situation to do so.

Now let's say you are at home recuperating from the same accident. Who would you like to have come and bring you comfort? The doctor because she is a medical professional? Of course not. The apostle/prophet? Not if it is supernatural comfort you are looking for. If you want insight into the life and spiritual implications of the event, the apostle/prophet is the one. But that is not what you are looking for. You would want the person endowed with the caring gift! The circumstance determines whose *functional authority* rules.

Let's say a married couple is having a dispute over who should control the family checkbook, the man or the woman. The husband says he should because he is the man, the head of the woman and the supposed head of the family and that is a man's job. Do you believe that is God's order for the family? Not necessarily. Let's say the husband barely passed eighth grade math and the wife works as a CPA. Who has authority to handle the checkbook? The wife! Her giftedness and training empowers her and has given her authority. Her functional authority takes precedence over any other perceived authority structures. Her training determines her sphere of authority, not some preconceived notions about gender "roles" that are "God-ordained." The Bible says nothing about which gender should handle the finances in the family. It is only prejudicial cultural bias that thinks it is the domain of men.

Once there was a senator flying first class across the country. On the same flight was a petite, 120-pound stewardess who was on her first day on the job. The plane was about to take off and she noticed the senator's seat belt was unbuckled. The bulky senator was engaged in an intense conversation with his seatmate and was ignoring the stewardess's instructions to buckle the belt. The stewardess politely and firmly approached the senator and asked him to buckle up. He responded, "Don't you know who I am?" She responded back: "Don't you know who I am? I have authority to keep this plane on the ground until you comply with my instruction!" That petite stewardess had the destiny of the whole plane in her hand! In that arena, her functional authority superseded the senator's positional authority.

A husband works as an electrical engineer. The wife grew up on a farm, working around heavy equipment all her life. The husband has never lifted anything heavier than a pencil and a calculator his entire life. The wife literally ran the farm during her father's prolonged illness. Let's say the family car breaks down or needs maintenance. Who has "authority" to do the job? The male because mechanical things are "divinely ordered" by God in the domain of the man? How absurd. Of course, the woman has authority because her experience and training qualify her for it!

The children's professionally-trained and gifted children's ministry worker is in conflict with a family in your church concerning children's curriculum. The family believes publisher A's material should be used as being far superior in their mind. The children's supervisor is using publisher B's material. You are the pastor who does not have a lick of children's ministry grace in your bones. Who should have "authority" over the children's ministry curriculum? The one who is functionally responsible and gifted. Because I may be the pastor does not give me the right to make policy decisions in areas for which I am not suited merely by reason of holding my office. Now, every analogy is limited, and a pastor might want to review for doctrinal accuracy, etc, but if pushed into a conflict, assuming other issues are where they should be, it is the pastor who should be ready to yield to the functional authority of the person with the gift for it. If the pastor cannot trust the judgment of the ministry supervisor, other issues need to be addressed.

Properly recognizing functional authority is instrumental in facilitating a quality team atmosphere. Football serves as another metaphor. How often do teams brutally fight it out in the mud and trenches for four quarters of blood, sweat, and tears, only to have the game decided by a 150-pound guy with a clean uniform—the field goal kicker—providing the victory. Do the other teammates resent him? With the game on the line, would you want the captain of your team, an exhausted three-hundred-pound interior lineman, doing the kicking just because of his rank? Of course not. He does not have functional authority for the job.

You may laugh at the simplicity of these analogies, but in all earnestness, relationships break down when the emphasis is on certain authority role prescriptions rather than acknowledging functional authority. I propose that every hour of every day there is grief, pain, hurt, abuse, and confusion happening in the Lord's church, caused by people who either do not understand the principle of functional authority or who are too insecure to acknowledge it.

Flowing in functional authority keeps the issue of honoring and respecting leaders in a "checked and balanced" state. "Professional" ministerial functions[17] such as pastor, teacher, apostle, prophet, elder, etc., are delegated functions. They are the King's delegates, acting under His authority. However these delegated positions do not supersede our functional authority as fellow members of the brotherhood/body. Therefore, delegated authority must submit to functional authority.

Sometime, if you are interested, examine the number of references in the New Testament to "brothers/brotherhood/one another" and compare it to the references to "elder or elders." It will be self-evident to you that the Scriptures emphasis is on the mutuality of brotherhood over delegated office. One's function in the body supersedes one's delegated positioning.

Delegated Authority

This is the first level at which any mortal has authority in relationship to another mortal on earth. Delegated authority is not necessarily dependent on age, ability, training, or giftedness but assignment from higher authority. The ideal situation exists when delegated authority matches functional authority, but it is often not the case and does not have to be so.

It would be unwise for a ninety-pound weakling to stand in the middle of the road facing an oncoming car with his hand in the air expecting traffic to stop. However, dress the same weakling in a blue uniform and give him a badge and traffic will stop. Why? It is not just because we know that we are dealing with a police officer. The reason we stop is because, as a society, we have delegated authority to the officer and the badge is a recognizable symbol of delegated authority. The officer doesn't have to be bigger, badder, meaner, or stronger. His receipt of delegated authority qualifies him to prevail.

Jesus has all authority in His person and has delegated it to His church. First it is to individual believers as fellow heirs and partners with Him in His victory over death, hell, and the grave. The believer is the extension of Christ's life and ministry in the earth. Many excellent volumes that deal in-depth with the believers' authority are readily available. I will not delve in to the matter here. The Ephesians 4:11–13 ministries and presbyters, or elders, are delegated authority.

In addition to each individual believer, the Lord has delegated authority to elders (presbyters/bishops) in the church. The details of the boundaries and limitations of delegated church authority will be discussed in chapters 6 and 7. Delegated authority is not about domination and control. It is about assuming the responsibility for guiding into destiny and fulfillment from a posture of care. Delegated authority never extends beyond the sphere of caring responsibility for which someone has been endowed by the Spirit to fulfill. Delegated authority is only activated in an area where I have responsibility, and it also follows responsibility. Authority without responsibility promotes tyranny. Responsibility without authority promotes frustration and discouragement. How does delegated authority work at a practical local church level? Let's consider a few hypothetical scenarios.

Pastor Jones is the senior pastor of the First Church of Anytown, USA, a mega-church of two thousand in attendance on Sunday. In his fellowship, he has a faithful member, Brother Jimmy. Brother Jimmy only has a fifth-grade education, but he has the spirit of helps and service. Looking to help Brother Jimmy have a sense of purpose and ministry, Pastor Jones makes him the overseer of the ushers responsible for the parking lot ministry. Jimmy takes to it like a moth to light and runs the parking lot like a well-oiled machine.

In May of that year, Pastor Jones schedules apostle Smith for a series of special meetings. Apostle Smith has forty-five years of ministry experience in international spheres. On the Friday night of the first meeting, apostle Smith pulls up to the church in his new Cadillac with two angels riding shotgun for him on the hood of the car. He parks in the row reserved for the children's ministry workers. He gets out of his car, and Brother Jimmy approaches him to move the car out of the reserved spot. The request puts off apostle Smith. After all, he is an apostle, worthy of honor. Jimmy persists: the car must be moved. The scene escalates slightly, and pastor Jones comes running to the scene and tells Jimmy it is all right for the apostle to park there. Jimmy walks away discouraged.

In this scenario who should have submitted to whom and why? The apostle has superior rank, ministry, calling, abilities, honor, and status. Jimmy should yield to the greater anointing and honor the man of God! *Yes?—No!*

Jimmy is functionally suited for the task, and his local ministry delegated the parking ministry to him. Jimmy's functional and delegated authority outranks the apostle's positional and ministerial authority at two levels! The parking lot was the sphere of the exercise of his authority, and anyone who enters it must submit to Jimmy. The apostle must move his car. Jimmy is under delegated authority; the apostle is not. Brother Smith's worldwide apostleship has absolutely no authority in the sphere of Jimmy's responsibility and delegated authority. The visiting apostle has no functional or delegated authority in the assembly other than that given to him by the pastor. Therefore, the apostle must yield to Jimmy by moving his car.

By failing to support Jimmy in this situation, the pastor has shown that he is a man-pleaser. He is impressed with rank and position rather than his own delegated authority decisions. Rather than pulling rank and nullifying his previous delegation, he should have commended Jimmy for having more spiritual acumen than the visiting guest apostle who is impressed with his rank and title. He has just cut Jimmy off at the knees. At the next local elders meeting, after Jimmy has taken his family and left the church hurt, the pastor will undoubtedly describe Jimmy as someone who did not understand authority. When in fact, it is the pastor who did not understand authority.

Sometimes insecure individuals in a church violate the principle of honoring delegated authority by not following chain of command in crisis or complaint. By doing an "end run" around appropriate delegated authority, the insecure individual will try to appeal to the pastor instead of the delegated authority to air a grievance or resolve a problem. Often the insecure individual will appeal to the positional authority of the pastor to avoid dealing with the difficulties of relational interaction with subordinate delegated authorities. A pastor who wants to help himself will not play into this dynamic out of a misguided sense of caring, helping, or wanting to be a listening ear.

Authority of Custom

"When in Rome, do as the Romans do."

In American culture, the above cliché means a person should adapt to one's surroundings, culture, and customs when visiting another country. This quote is from patristic literature. It was the advice given by the church fathers to Christians who asked how they should behave when visiting a church that did not share the same practices as their own.

Every local church has its own distinctives, emphases, and calling. These are the sovereign choices of the Holy Spirit—wonderful to behold and a participatory joy. However, each local church often has *unspoken* expectations of how a Christian should "behave." They are those values and practices, not biblically explicit, which, for better or worse, are expected of individuals in the local congregation.

Paul was very sensitive to matters of local culture. He did not expect congregations in different geographic areas to necessarily have the same sensibilities on all issues. The matter of women's head coverings in 1 Corinthians 11 is a classic example. Many today often ignore the most important part of the entire passage: "We have no such custom, neither do the churches of God."[18]

What was Paul saying? He was dealing with the authority of custom in Corinth, trying to navigate the delicate waters of the freedom of the

New Covenant with propriety of local custom. It was a "local" issue that did not apply to other churches. I once read a "theological paper" from a scholar on the issue of the permanence of women's head coverings, arguing that it is a universal and timeless "law of God." In about fifteen pages of commentary, the author never mentioned the most important verse! This is the type of biased, prejudicial teaching on authority and covering that does harm in the church. Our Christian liberty needs to yield to local custom when a potential conflict arises.

God help us to submit to the true higher authorities in His church and in the world.

PART 2

THE VIEW FROM THREE INCHES

CHAPTER 4

DEFINITIONAL
DIGGING

In the previous chapters, we examined biblical authority from a thematic and philosophical perspective. The time has come for some textual plowing in the Scriptures. I realize a good portion of humanity does not have much appetite for the details of biblical language word studies. It is as thrilling for some as a root canal without Novocain. However, there is simply no getting around the need. Salvation is simple. A four-year-old can understand enough to be converted. However, rightly handling the Scriptures and correctly applying its teachings to our lives is not as easy. It requires work. While not attempting to build a skyscraper of biblical brilliance here, it is necessary we roll up our sleeves a bit and at least turn over a few shovelfuls of exegetical dirt. Chapters 5–7 of this book will examine the more practical local church applications of these authority and submission issues. Perhaps they will be more immediately relevant to readers and a bit less brain-stretching and tedious than some of this chapter.

So, grab your hard hat and watch out for falling rock. Stick with me for some foundational digging. Perhaps we can turn over a theological rock or two, lay a brick of new insight here and there, and potentially put in the foundation for a completely new building.

Church expression concerning authority and submission ranges from dictatorial authoritarianism to lawless libertinism.[1] It is impossible to have discourse without agreement on definition of terms. Coloring the definition and usage of these terms with contemporary cultural values is a serious weakness in traditional teaching on authority, submission, and headship.

When your marriage is under assault, your children are going crazy, and your finances are in the tank, Greek definitions may seem as relevant as a camel in Siberia. However, conforming our lives to God's Word requires accuracy. Theology is seriously relevant business. If we are going to establish new thinking on the subject, we need to closely reexamine some language. So, in this chapter we will examine the meaning and usage of Greek words[2] translated in the King James Version as *command, ordain, order, rule, obey, submit, head/headship*, and *authority over*.

Clearing Our Culture

If we are going to lay a new foundation, the first thing we need to do before we can even dig is remove the underbrush of culture from the land. The New Testament uses several different words related to authority and submission. It is important to understand each, to know its definition, usage, *and* limitations. Unfortunately, many times, English translations are neither consistent nor clear but rather contradictory. Confusion frequently results from the imposition of modern Western cultural values onto biblical terms, which gives them meaning the authors of Scripture *never intended*. We all bring cultural bias to the biblical text. As Westerners, we bring our individualist, capitalist, imperialist culture and corporate business mindset to the Scriptures. These are serious detriments to correct understanding of the Word. Part of the chore associated with understanding Scripture is trying, as best we can, to recognize this tendency and avoid it.

We must understand what words meant to those who heard and read them before we try to apply them to our circumstances. This is called the interpretive principle of originality. What did the author *intend?* What did his hearers *understand?* How did they *apply* it? Only after we have established these in some degree of accuracy can we apply the Scriptures to ourselves. Failure here has serious consequences. In local churches I have pastored, I often joked that I would die a happy man if my tombstone read: "He got God's people to pay attention to context and culture!" Don't preach or teach a verse apart from its context, and pay attention to culture. Don't read ours into it, and don't transfer theirs out of it! We will start by looking at the English word, *command.*

Command

Are believers required to obey the commands and instruction of their leaders? How and to what degree? Does a leader, particularly an apostle, have the right to expect or require compliance with his leadership? If yes, are there any limitations?

There are several different words translated as *command* in the King James Version. Here they are with abbreviated definitions:[3]

- *epō*: say, utter
- *entellomai*: enjoin, charge, command, direct, give orders, ordain
- *protassō*: determine beforehand, ordain
- *epitassō*: arrange upon, order, align, command, charge, enjoin
- *keleuō*: urge on, incite
- *paraggellō*: transmit a message, enjoin, declare, urge

The Scripture uses only *two* of these to describe interactions between believers and their leaders: *epitassō* and *keleuō*.

Epitassō **(Philemon 8).** Only Philemon 8 uses *epitassō* inter-relationally between believers. Paul refers to his right to require compliance in the conflict between Onesimus and Philemon. Although Paul claims the right, *he declines to use it,* choosing rather to appeal to love. This has significant bearing on the whole issue of apostolic authority. I am alarmed and discouraged that so much of the current discourse in the apostolic movement is focused on the authority of the apostles. For example:

> I do not want to overstress this, but viewing an apostle through the grid of authority is essential.[4] Either apostles do have authority over the church on behalf of Christ or they do not. If apostles do have authority, then the church needs to listen to them.[5]

I believe this is a mistake. If we emphasize the authority of the apostolic leader, executive privileges, rank, etc. over Calvary love, we have at least failed the test of a Pauline spirit if not the letter of Pauline doctrine.[6] The context of Paul's letter to Philemon was *a life and death matter!*[7] With issues of that magnitude at stake, it makes sense to speak and act with "command authority." However, *it is a mistake* to: a) base doctrine or method on singular proof texts, and b) make normative that which is intended for crisis!

Paraggellō (**1 Corinthians 7:10, 11:17; 1 Thessalonians 4:11; 2 Thessalonians 3:4, 6, 10, 12; 1 Timothy 1:3, 4:11, 5:7, 6:13, 17**). In 1 Corinthians 11:17, *paraggellō* simply means "declaring a truth or transmitting a message from another source." In 1 Corinthians 7:10, Paul is likewise simply transmitting a message as from the Lord. Paul is speaking as the Lord's very representative, with authority, to a moral issue. Paul is very discreet in his writings when he is aware and believes himself speaking with immediate divine unction. He is careful to differentiate his "leadership counsel" from the word of the Lord.[8] We would do well to do the same. Speaking with authoritative command was not Paul's normal method. He reserved it primarily for correcting doctrinal or behavioral (sin) issues.

In 1 Thessalonians 4:11 and 2 Thessalonians 3:4,6,10, and 12, Paul uses *paraggellō* in the same general exhortation to the same people on the same issue. These verses primarily deal two situations in

Thessalonica that appear to be local: conformity to apostolic doctrine and the sin of laziness.

In 1 Timothy 1:3, 4:11, 5:7, 6:13, 17, Paul enjoins and empowers a younger Timothy concerning instruction in areas of core doctrine and behavior: Gnostic incursion,[9] care of widows, defending the faith, and the deceitfulness of riches. He is taking his apostolic authority transmitted to him from the Lord and transmitting it to Timothy to teach apostolic doctrine with authority.

From this simple analysis, we see there is no biblical basis for expecting a believer to unilaterally submit to a leader based on the King James Version rendering of *command*. Being in right relationship to a leader does not mean a perennial posture of deference and approval seeking for every decision of life, supposedly for "safety's sake."[10] Leaders have command authority for doctrinal and moral/behavioral issues that are explicitly sin. Other than that, their role is advice and counsel.

Ordain and Order

There are a couple of Greek words that the King James Version translates as *ordain* or *order*. Though not technically the same as command, they are authoritative and worth examining. They are:

- *diatassō*: ordain, appoint, give order, set in order
- *epidorthoō*: order, to set in order

DIATASSŌ (**1 Corinthians 7:17, 9:14, 11:34, 16:1; Galatians 3:19; Titus 1:5**). Paul uses this term in the Galatians passage to describe the activity of angels. For our purposes regarding local church issues it is not relevant. This is also the case in 1 Corinthians 9:14 where the term refers to the Lord's own personal authority. No one disputes that. What is the context of the remaining four passages?

- 1 Corinthians 7:17: instruction on Christian liberty and moral behavior regarding marriage

- 1 Corinthians 11:34: bringing order out of chaos and carnality at the "communion," or Eucharist, meal
- 1 Corinthians 16:1: handling money for an offering
- Titus 1:5: ordaining elders (in Crete)

It is significant that this term is *only found* in Paul's communications with Corinth and Crete. They had something in common: gross disorder and dysfunction. In Crete, there were many unruly people (abominable, disobedient, and reprobate) putting forth grievous false doctrine (affecting entire households), fables, and Jewish mythology, all for the love of money.[11] When one of your own poets says your god is your belly, it is not a compliment.[12] The situation in Crete was doctrinal and moral corruption. The situation in Corinth was worse. For all their spirituality, the Corinthian church was the poster child for church dysfunction. The entire letter is basically nonstop correction in one form or another.

Paul uses *diatassō* to describe his apostolic role of bringing young, emergent, and seriously dysfunctional churches into alignment with apostolic doctrine, ethics, and moral behavior. This is legitimate apostolic function. On fundamental gospel issues and in the presence of gross moral and doctrinal disorder, it is appropriate for apostles, or anyone else for that matter, to exercise authority to bring order. However, the *circumstances limit the scope.*

It is exegetically illegitimate to make *normative* that which is *exceptional.* Authority standards, methods, models, structures, philosophies, ethics, etc. designed for abominable, disobedient, and reprobate people *do not apply* to believers who do not fall into those categories! You do not use a screwdriver to drive a nail. (Unless you are like me and have lost the hammer and don't want to bother looking for it!) It is a *legitimate tool* that *does not apply* to the need or circumstance. *Diatassō* authority is functionally and circumstantially *limited.*

Even conformity to apostolic authority in doctrine is *limited* to core gospel truths, not secondary biblical themes and "revelations"[13] that an apostle (or any teacher) may present and teach at a given moment. All Christians must yield to the core apostolic teaching of *I preach Christ and Him crucified*. However, other thematic teachings must be scrutinized and kept or tossed based on their alignment to the core message.

Ability to discern core alignment is rare in American Christian culture of low biblical literacy (in both pulpit and pew) where religious performance and legalism abound. In charismatic circles, we routinely preach preference, themes, topics, typology, things, "isms," dreams, visions, and "new revelations" as doctrine to the neglect of the core gospel message. Doctrinal drift and bizarre behavioral codes are the inevitable result. The notion is absurd that believers must yield to or submit in an awestruck manner to whatever pops out of an apostle's mouth simply because he is an apostle.

Some believe expanding spheres of authority define the apostolic dimension.[14] Rather than believing for *expanded* spheres of apostolic authority, the apostolic movement needs to seek ways to *restrain* carnal and ambitious apostolic authority, which frequently masquerades as being visionary.[15] Apostolic authority must be limited to its biblical dimensions.

This is a significant point. Much written and taught today concerning the apostolic movement insists that believers must stay "apostolically aligned" to "their covering apostle" in order to be blessed and under God's favor and spiritual protection. The divine purpose of apostolic authority is to keep the believer *Christ-aligned,* living in the realities of the New Covenant and morally clean. It is not to assure personal alignment with the apostle bringing the instruction! "Biblical alignment," if one wants to use the term, is to Christ, through a ministry, *not to the person* or the "*office.*" Paul *rebuked* the Corinthians for their thinking of alignment unto certain men: I am of Paul, I am of Apollos, etc.[16] Let me modernize it a bit: Apostle ———— is my covering. Apostle ———— is my authority. Apostle ———— is my spiritual father.

It is illegitimate and a wrenching out of context to use these verses for an alleged permanent order of apostolic covering where believers and churches must be beholden to a covering apostle. The passages say nothing about an obligatory system whereby one's spiritual covering must pre-approve personal life decisions. An apostle is not the chief executive of the church or network. Spiritual jeopardy does not categorically result from failure to get apostolic sanction and blessing on the routine decisions of life in God. A leader's counseling role is not to tell the other person what to do but to teach him/her how to touch Christ by the Spirit. The leader's role is not to provide sanction or non-sanction for a seeker but to facilitate a divine encounter that enables godly decision making and to blow the whistle on overt sin when present. The level of exercised apostolic authority should *diminish*, not expand, in proportion to the maturity of the saint or church.

Apostolic authority is not a static quality vested in an office; it is a functional grace, activated by the Holy Spirit as needed for the people and circumstance that need it. When the foundation is done, the apostle needs to get out of the way, not retain executive authority over the church (es) as he attempts to build the financial infrastructure to support himself.

Epidorthoō (**Titus 1:5**). The fact that Scripture uses this word only once should tell us a little about the limitation of its scope. Again, the context is significant. It deals with the situation in Crete where from stump-worshipping, unruly pagans Paul was trying to raise a church. It derives from a root word with the thought of "straightening out." In American culture, an *ortho*dontist straightens teeth. You can see the same word root, *ortho*. The thought seems to be that Paul left some straightening undone. He commissions Titus to finish the job. No problem—as long as the alignment is to Christ and not to the apostle himself or alleged revelations he may have on subordinate issues. The church at Crete needed serious straightening. But just as when the teeth are straight you remove the braces, so apostolic authority and influence needs to be lifted and removed when the job is done, not held and exercised in perpetuity through office or rank. The apostle, if he is one, needs to move on.

Rule

The King James Version translates different Greek words as *rule, rule over,* or *ruler*:

- *kanōn:* a measure or rule, sphere of influence, or limit, guide
- *brabeuō:* act as umpire, arbitrate, govern, rule
- *archōn:* first in rank or power and authority, chief, preeminent, ruler
- *poimainō:* shepherd, be a shepherd
- *proistēmi:* go before, to lead, to stand before, preside over, rule
- *hēgeomai:* lead or command with official authority, have authority over
- *kathistēmi:* appoint, designate, set, rule, constitute, conduct

The New Testament never uses *kanōn, brabeuō,* and *archōn* to describe any relationship between believers or with their leaders. *Kathistēmi* is used only once (in Titus 1:5) in relationship to church governmental order (please refer to the previous paragraphs). The New Testament uses *archōn* or *archē* in reference to civic and secular authorities and demonic powers, but *never* in regard to *any* relationship within the church, including church authority, positions, offices, husband/wife relationships, parent/child relationships, and believers to leaders or vice versa. *Archon is never used* in the New Testament describing any relationship between believers. The concept of one person ruling over another in a local assembly should never be among us.

***Poimainō* means literally "to shepherd."** The thought is "going before, leading," not "sitting over" or ruling in a hierarchal sense of superiority due to office or rank. Overseeing shepherds lead and feed, they do not rule over subordinates.[17] *Proistēmi* (1 Thessalonians 5:12; 1 Timothy 3:4, 5, 12, 5:17; Titus 3:8, 14) is almost the same. It means "to go or stand *before*" (Gr. prefix: *pros*) not "*over*" (Gr. Prefix: *epi*). It means "to preside, to act out, perform, to produce," not "rule over."

Wait a minute, Crosby, doesn't the Scripture say we are to obey them that have the rule over us?[18] It can't be any plainer than that! Before authoritarians everywhere jump up and say, "See, I told you so!" We best examine the context of this verse: To whom was the author speaking? In what location? About what? Why?

HĒGEOMAI (translated as *rule* in Hebrews 13:7, 17, 24). Let's use the synthesis principle (letting Scripture interpret Scripture). The Hebrew epistle was written to Jewish believers facing extreme disappointment in their faith. They were in crisis. They were under the duress of physical persecution. The delay of the return of the Lord left them wavering in their faith. They were considering abandoning their new Christian faith and returning to Judaism. The context of the Hebrews passages is one of *crisis* and *apostasy*. The matter is one of concern for their souls: a life and death, salvation, or perdition issue.

These verses in Hebrews are the *only place* the King James Version translates *hēgeomai* as *rule*. It is translated elsewhere with the connotation of "esteeming, to evaluate, judge, to count or consider" something. In a situation of persecution, impending disaster, mass backsliding, or apostasy, it is appropriate to use the term and to speak of leaders authoritatively. Using the Hebrews verses normatively when similar circumstances do not exist is *inappropriate* and *exegetically illegitimate*.

The concept of an eternal subordinancy of one believer to another as some sort of "spiritual covering" is alien to the norm of the New Testament. The exception is in times of corporate crisis when someone's eternal soul, the welfare of the entire body, or partnership in the gospel is at stake.

Obey and Obedience

Can we salvage these terms from Old Covenant, hierarchal, authoritarian, controlling abuse; and contemporary, reactionary, independent, rebellious anarchy? Let's try. As in our other examinations, there are different Greek words translated as *obey/obedience* in the New Testament: They are

- *peithō:* to persuade, convince by argument, pacify, trust, conciliate, assent, agree to, obey
- *peitharchō:* persuade, or be convinced by a ruler
- *ginomai:* (used once in King James Version) cause to come into being
- *hupakouō:* listen attentively, hear, give heed, conform to, obey
- *hupakoē:* obedience, compliance, submission

The New Testament never uses *peitharchō* and *ginomai* in regard to the relationship between believers and their leaders. The King James Version inconsistently translates *peithō*. "To trust, or to have confidence, or to be persuaded" are the most common and frequent King James Version renderings. We are to trust, have confidence in, and yield to our leaders, especially in crisis, but not unilaterally obey them. The King James Version translators projected their relationship to their king onto church relationships, and we have suffered for it ever since. In Galatians 3:1 and 5:7, believers are told to obey *peithō, the truth*—a most appropriate rendering. We owe the truth absolute obedience but not our leaders.

The word, *hupakouō*, expresses the believer's relationship to God or the gospel but *not one another or leaders*. There are exceptions in two verses: Philippians 2:12 and 2 Thessalonians 3:14. In these two passages it means to "attentively listen to and yield to" core gospel doctrine and moral instruction–Pauline preaching. It does not describe a relationship of rank: someone superior to another, one who must yield to another. The New Testament exhorts children and slaves to obey (*hupakouō*)[19] but not believers to leaders, nor wives to husbands. The significance of the absence of this word has profound implications on the whole submission to authority issue. Unilateral submission to a leader simply because he or she is one *does not exist in the New Testament.* Yielding to core gospel doctrine and moral injunctions does. A fixed position of relational subservience does not.

On the negative side, the Scriptures refer to disobedience. It is the Greek word *apeitheia:* "disbelief, obstinate, and rebellious." The King James Version also translates it as *unbelief.* In the post-Pentecost era, the New Testament never uses it in reference to believers.[20] The Scriptures think more highly of believers than most of us do. There is only one New Testament use of *parakoē* (in 2 Corinthians 10:6), meaning "inattentive listening," implying disobedience. The passage contrasts the believer's obedience with the inattentive disobedience of those whose minds are exalted against the knowledge of God. It is not referring to the disobedience of the believers but of the high-minded unbeliever, judgment upon them being contingent upon the believer's obedience.

Submit and Submission

The word used in the New Testament for *submit* and *submission* is very unique and worth careful examination. It is *hupotassō.* It means "to order, align, or arrange under, to subject." It comes from a root military word meaning the alignment or arrangement of troops. It is not commonly found in Greek literature but is quite common in Greek papyri describing business transactions where it means "to support, append, or uphold." The idea is of what we might call an appendix or addendum, something added to a document or transaction to "support" the main document.[21]

The King James Version does not consistently translate the term. Sometimes it is *submit, submission,* or *subjection*; sometimes, *obey/obedience.* It does not mean obedience. Obedience is related to conduct, and it is relative, never absolute. Submission is related to heart attitude, which is absolute. I can be submissive and yet not obey. The New Testament requires only children and slaves to obey. Believers (wives *and* husbands) are required to submit. Submission is an attitude or posture of yieldedness, not categorical compliance to authority. This is the requirement and distinctive of freedom. Only slaves and children can be compelled because of their status. They are not free. Free people can submit, but they never cannot be compelled to obey. Slaves obey because demand requires it. Sons obey because it is in their submissive, compliant nature to do so.

The only active usage of *hupotassō* in the New Testament in an authoritative and mandatory sense is in reference to God's own activity and in Luke 10 where the believer's authority requires demons to submit. Indeed, God has the right to require others to unconditionally submit. Believers can require demons to submit. We may not require one another to submit. In a Christian and biblical context, the best renderings for hupotassō would connote "yieldedness, compliance, support, deference, agreeable, non-combative," rather than "aggressive resistance." Try reading the many familiar submit and submission passages inserting these words instead of "obey and subject" and see the effect it has on your understanding (e.g. 1 Peter 5:5; Ephesians 5:21).

Biblically, *hupotasso* is a "self-surrender," a readiness to renounce one's own will for the sake of others. It does not just apply to females and wives. It applies to everyone. To recognize the other person as Christ's own representative and to conduct yourself accordingly, recognizing and submitting to the Christ in one another.

Believers must obey their leaders in matters of doctrinal conformity and moral issues. Even then, only in crisis and conflict. The rest of the time believers submit: voluntarily looking for and yielding to Christ in one another and their leaders. God alone receives *unqualified obedience* without measure; any person lower than God can only receive *qualified submission*.

Head and Headship

When it comes to the biblical terms *head* and *headship*, we run into a situation of conflicting metaphors. Different cultures use different body metaphors to explain things. In Western cultures, our heart is the seat of our affections. In the biblical Semitic culture, it was the bowels. In the Philippines, when you love some one, he/she has "captured your liver." "Fat" is a compliment in the Philippines, meaning "healthy, vibrant, full of life," very similar to a Semitic view of "fatness" as something positive. Not so in Western culture! In American culture, we have "smart mouths" meaning "sassy obstinate, resistive, or non-compliant." In Semitic culture, the forehead (i.e. having a whore's forehead) was a metaphor for the same. In Western culture, the head speaks of executive authority and rulership: e.g. the "head" of an organization being the singular chief executive endued with authority, if not absolute authority. That is because, in the West, we think, act, decide, "will" from our brain/head. Therefore, for us, the head "logically" represents executive decision-making authority. Where did the people of Scripture believe executive authority resided? Here is a brief survey.

- Genesis 6:5: "And GOD saw that the wickedness of man *was* great in the earth, and *that* every imagination of the thoughts of his heart *was* only evil continually."
- Job 31:7: "If my step hath turned out of the way, and mine heart walked after mine eyes, and if any blot hath cleaved to mine hands."
- Proverbs 4:23: "Keep thy heart with all diligence; for out of it *are* the issues of life."
- Proverbs 8:5: "O ye simple, understand wisdom: and, ye fools, be ye of an understanding heart."
- Proverbs 14:33: "Wisdom resteth in the heart of him that hath understanding: but *that which is* in the midst of fools is made known."
- Proverbs 16:9: "A man's heart deviseth his way: but the LORD directeth his steps."
- Proverbs 23:7: "For as he thinketh in his heart, so is he: Eat and drink, saith he to thee; but his heart is not with thee."
- Psalms 27:8: "*When thou saidst*, Seek ye my face; my heart said unto thee, Thy face, LORD, will I seek."
- Matthew 15:19: "For out of the heart proceed evil thoughts, murders, adulteries, fornications, thefts, false witness, blasphemies. . . ."

For Semites, *the heart*, representing the whole of a person, *not the head*, was the seat of executive authority. It is a mistake to read our culture into the biblical text. Before we can make any principle of application to ourselves, we need to apply the principles of context, culture, and originality and ask how the people of the time understood the head metaphor.

In Hebrew, the word translated as *head* is *ro'sh*. The Hebrew Old Testament translates *ro'sh* as "chief, leader, tribal leader, superior in authority" about 180 times. The LXX[22] rarely uses the Greek *kephalé* when translating the Hebrew *ro'sh* (approximately five percent of the time),[23] but rather prefers *archon* or *archē*, which we earlier saw, never describe the relationship between believers. *Kephalé* likely derives from the root, *kapto*, meaning "to seize." It literally means that which is most easily seized because of its *prominence*, not its rank.[24] The New Testament uses it literally for our noggin, because, well, it sticks out; not because it rules our body!

Though not common, *kephalé* can also mean "source or origin."[25] As hard as it may be for us to believe or understand, the ancients believed that semen came from the male brain (the head). For them the head represented the source of life. Aristotle taught this and influenced generations after him. Because of this belief, the Romans euphemistically referred to sexual intercourse as "diminishing one's head."[26]

Christ is head of the church. Using the synthesis principle again, let's allow Scripture to interpret Scripture. There are seven explicit New Testament verses that speak of Christ's headship. How do they explicitly relate to executive authority, government, ruling, and order?

> And he is the head (*kephalé*) of the body, the church: who is the beginning, the firstborn from the dead; that in all things he might have the preeminence.
>
> (Colossians 1:18)

What does this verse (and its context) say about government or ruling? *Nothing.* Christ is the exalted originator and completer by reason of His work, He is "preeminent."

> And not holding the Head (*kephalé*), from which all the body by joints and bands having nourishment ministered, and knit together, increaseth with the increase of God.
>
> (Colossians 2:19)

What does this verse say about ruling, authority over, or government? *Nothing.* His headship is defined in terms of sustainer, originator, and nourisher of life.

> But speaking the truth in love, may grow up into him in all things, which is the head, even Christ. From whom the whole body fitly joined together and compacted by that which every joint supplieth, according to the effectual working in the measure of every part, maketh increase of the body unto the edifying of itself in love.
>
> (Ephesians 4:15–16)

What does this verse say about ruling, authority over, or government? *Nothing.* This passage stresses the unity of the head and body and Christ as the nourisher and sustainer of growth and life

> But I would have you know, that the head of every man is Christ; and the head of the woman is the man; and the head of Christ *is* God.
>
> (1 Corinthians 11:3)

What does this verse say about, ruling, authority over, or government? *Nothing.* You must read into the meaning of head and see something that is not there. This is a notoriously difficult passage. If we substitute "authority over" for "head" and read the passage, *it makes no sense. God is not in authority over Christ*, neither is the man "authority over" the woman.

There is no rank or hierarchy in the Godhead! There are not conflicted wills requiring one executive God making sure the other subordinate God stays in alignment with His will! Such thoughts are pagan (and too often believed by Christians!). Where there is only one will, there is no need for authority. Authority exists only in an atmosphere where alternate wills are possible. God is not conflicted within Himself, within His persons.[27] Authority and submission structures are designed for the angels and humanity as a result of satan's and Adam's fall. They are necessary in an atmosphere where *agape* does not rule one hundred percent of the time and where independent self-will is a possibility. They are not eternal orders or operation the Trinity self-imposes to keep one another in line! *How absurd!*

In the marriage relationship (Ephesians 5:21ff.) for example, authority and submission are the "fall-back position" necessary to maintain order when love fails. They are a necessary fruit of the fall, not a mirror of the Trinity's essential nature. There are twice as many exhortations to the husband to love as there are to the wife to submit. When Calvary love fails, authority and submission are necessary to keep order. This does not mean the female unilaterally submits to the male because of gender-based, role theology. It means that if the husband and wife cannot find unity, the husband's job is to manifest selfless Calvary love (not executive authority), and the wife is to submit to it: *as Christ is to the Church.*

Christ is indeed the sovereign of the church *because He laid his life down for her and continues to broker life to her.* Christ's own "authority" is conditioned on His willingness to embrace death and release life. Though He was King from eternity, He was "vested" with His rights in the resurrection, because He was willing to taste death (Philippians 2:6–11). In a limited sense, He "earned" His rulership as sovereign, though sovereign from eternity past. It is not unlike a prince taking the throne. A prince is a prince by reason of birth. But there comes a day when, educated and hopefully proven, He takes the throne. He is "vested" with the authority that was always his by reason of birth. In this limited metaphorical sense, Christ was "given" a name above every other to whom all will bow. Why? *Because of His willingness to taste death for every man.* Excuse me a moment of worship: *Glory to God! Hallelujah, I am rescued! What a great king, lover, and friend!*

That is the correct image for the husband in the marriage relationship, not "authority over and ruling" because I am the male and males rule! Love and self-sacrifice are the "norm" for the marriage relationship. Authority and submission are the guardrails of oneness when love fails. If a couple cannot find harmony, the husband's "point of view" is not the "final word" because he is the male and the executive head. *Both individuals must yield to higher authority*—submit to spiritual leadership in their crisis.

The church declared the doctrine of the eternal subordinancy of the Son[28] heresy two thousand years ago. It is experiencing a resurrection in some fundamentalist circles among authoritarians who believe that being male is equivalent to having role-based authority. It is also experiencing resurrection in apostolic restorationist circles among those who believe that an apostle possesses functional headship over others, supposedly like the Father does over Christ.[29] If *kephalé* (head) means "preeminent, source, or originator," as in the other verses, it makes more sense in its context. This verse does not mention submission. It must be read into it.

Isn't a woman supposed to be under authority and "covering"? We will talk about covering in the next chapter. Here, the word for *authority* is not passive. It is active. The authority "over" her head is *hers to exercise*; not someone else's to exercise over her. She has authority over her own head. In 1 Corinthians 11:10, the New International Version adds the phrase, "sign of," in its translation. It is not in the original language text, and is an unfortunate addition. First Corinthians 11:3 is not an authority hierarchy or flowchart. It is best understood as a sequential time line of origination, not rank or hierarchical spiritual covering.[30]

> For the husband is the head of the wife, even as Christ is the head of
> the church: and he is the Savior of the body.
>
> (Ephesians 5:23)

What does this verse say about ruling, authority over, or government? *Nothing*, unless you read "authority over" into the meaning of
"head" (*kephalé*). The context speaks of love and self-sacrifice, not a
word about ruling over. Neither *archon* nor *exousía* can be found in the
passage. They are simply not there. It must be read into the passage: a
case of classic eisegesis, if not pure fantasy.

> And hath put all things under his feet, and gave him to be the head
> over all things to the church . . . Which is his body, the fullness of
> him that filleth all in all.
>
> (Ephesians 1:22–23)

What does this verse contextually say about ruling, authority over, or
government? *Nothing*. It is, again, a head/body metaphor emphasizing
unity, oneness, exaltation, superiority, and preeminence. The context
(verses 20–23) is speaking of Christ being above all "authorities and
powers"; Christ's authority extends from crown to feet.

> For in him dwelleth all the fulness of the Godhead bodily. And ye are
> complete in him, which is the head of all principality and power....
>
> (Colossians 2:9–10)

Perhaps, in this verse, the concept of "authority over" might be legitimate. However, the context, again, is a head/body metaphor emphasizing
unity and oneness. In 2:10, a better rendering would be "top, crown, or
preeminent." Christ is preeminent because of His exalted position by
virtue of His cross and resurrection, and in His primacy and creatorship
He is the originator of even those spiritual powers that resist Him.

What is the end of this? If Christ's relationship to the church is the pattern for a husband and wife, and inferentially, leaders to the church, biblical headship has nothing to do with government and ruling. We must not mix cultural metaphors. For Semites, the head was the source of life, not the seat of government. The heart was the seat of government and ruling. *Kephalé* was rarely (five percent in the LXX) and uncommonly used for "leader or chief," but *never* "authority over" *(exousia)* or "ruling" *(arche)*. The best renderings connote the ideas of preeminence and, less strongly, "source or origin."

Authority Over

Exousía. This is the most significant of all the words related to our topic. It means "to have authority or authority over." It is an "abused" concept—on both extremes. Jesus is indeed, Lord. We are a part of a kingdom, not a democracy. This is inherently authoritative. However, the *kind* of authority the kingdom has and *how it is implemented* is the difference between something healthy and something abusive.

The word derives from the Greek *exesti:* it is lawful, meaning at its simplest level "to have ability, capacity to act, competency, to have leave, permission, power of choice, ability, or capability." Originally, *exousia* meant the liberty of doing as one pleases, which developed into the thought of the ability or strength with which one is endued. The King James Version translates it sometimes as *power,* sometimes as *authority*—unfortunate and confusing because of our language's connotations. Power in Greek is *dúnamis.* Authority is *exousía.* They are not the same. *Exousia* (authority) is the right to exercise *dúnamis* (power). Over time, the language changed and the meaning developed into the exercise of power and the power given to rulers.

How does the Scripture use *exousia?*

- It is used of secular rulers, civil authorities, and Gentiles (Luke 20:20, 19:17; Romans 13:1–3).

- Spoken of Christ (Revelation 12:10; Matthew 21:23, 24, 27, 28:18; etc.).
- Spoken of God (Jude 25).
- The potter has authority over the clay (Romans 9:21).
- The Beast "exercises" authority (Revelation 13:12).
- The two witnesses (Revelation 11:6).
- Christ's and the believer's "authority over" unclean spirits (Matthew 10:1; Mark 6:7).
- Individual believer's conscience (1 Corinthians 7:37, 8:9; 2 Thessalonians 3:9; 1 Corinthians 6:12).
- Paul's authority to be married if he wished (1 Corinthians 9:5).

Did you notice anything *conspicuously absent?* Leaders "exercising authority over" believers and believers "exercising authority over" one another—it's not there. I know of one local church whose bylaws explicitly state that the pastor presides over the congregation like the president does over a country and that the members must obey the pastor as they would the president. It is alleged that apostles serve the same role over churches and networks. It is heartrending to see such a weak, illegitimate, and biblically unsustainable metaphor used to mislead and, yes, control God's people.

The Lord explicitly admonishes us not to use or model the world's thinking and methods in terms of government![31] President is to country as pastor is to church or apostle is to network *are not benign metaphors.* They are the philosophical seedbeds of abuse. Control with a smile, velvet-glove smoothness, charm and personality warmth is just as devilish as methods less sophisticated and aggressive. It makes it more devilish, as it is harder to recognize. Some of the "nicest" people in the church are control abusers.

Every time the word *exousía* is used in the New Testament in its verb form, it is active, not passive. You probably slept through seventh-grade grammar like I did. Let's try an accurate but simple definition. An active verb describes action being *done by* someone. A passive verb denotes action being *done to* someone. Try this: "Ignorance is considered by some people as a fault." This is passive. Fault is an object receiving another's consideration. Consideration is *acting upon* fault.

"People consider ignorance a fault." This is active. People *are doing their own considering*.

Both phrases convey the same thought, but one is passive and one active. Biblical authority is always active. It is something I possess and exercise, *not* something that is exercised *by* someone else *over* me.

I know that what I am presenting here sounds contrary to the prevailing teaching on this subject. Perhaps rallying some scholars whose brains exceed mine might help convince the reader that I am not endorsing some novel concept conjured up out of my inflated ego or in reaction to my own experience with abusive authority (I know some of you have been thinking that!). The italicized emphases are mine!

> But *exousia* means "authority" not "subjection"; when any one is said to have authority it *does not mean that the person is set under someone.* William Ramsay poured scorn on the idea that the term can indicate women's subjection, seeing this as a preposterous idea, which *a Greek scholar would laugh at anywhere except in the New Testament* (cited *in Robertson and Plummer*).

> For that they need authority and he is saying that their head covering is their sign of authority. As M.D. Hooker puts it, "Far from being a symbol of the woman's subjection to man, therefore, her head covering is what Paul calls it—authority: in prayer and prophecy she, like the man, is under the authority of God.[32]

Authority is like honor. It belongs to you. You can give it, but it cannot be demanded. You can give authority, and you can take it back. Submission can be received, not taken. Authority is not resident on a church officeholder. It is resident in the individual, who, from his or her volition may give it to those who are worthy of the individual's trust. This protects from victimization and abuse.[33] Before God, as a result of endowment and calling, a leader has "authority" in the sense of being accountable to God for those under his or her care: the leader has authority "over." But before the people, the leader is not over them but among them.[34]

Exceptions?

1. 1 Corinthians 7:3–6. Here Paul refers to authority in the sexual marriage relationship, at first glance seeming to imply that individuals do not possess authority. *Exousía* is indeed referred to. However, even here it is not as something one member "exercises" over another but as something both partners have to give away to the other! The context is the mutual exchange of authority, not the exercise of authority one over the other. The context is neither party has any *exousía*! This excludes, of course, abuse and defiling of conscience.

2. Matthew 8:5–13; Luke 7:1–10. Those who strongly emphasize submission to authority in the context of leadership often use the story of the centurion as justification of their view. Our Lord does not commend the centurion's submission to authority but rather the fact that the centurion recognizes Christ's delegated authority from the Father! Indeed, Christ has authority! The commendation is for the centurion's *faith, not submission to authority.* Submission to authority was the centurion's *point of reference* to faith and recognition of who Jesus was.

   Also, this scenario was pre-Pentecost (pre-new creation order) with a Gentile, someone who was not part of the covenant. Indeed, the Word says the Gentiles rule over one another! It is fine for them. It is not to be so among us.[35] Jesus was not endorsing some eternal principle of authority-submission order. He was commending the centurion for being able to "connect the dots" from his world to Christ's commission. Jesus was not endorsing Gentile structures of authority and submission as the model for His covenant community in the future era (after His resurrection). He was simply saying, paraphrased and in popular language: "I wish my own people could connect the dots and recognize who I am, the authority I have, and what my mission is like this guy!"

3. 2 Corinthians 10:8, 13:10. In the entire New Testament, these are the only two verses that speak of a leader and his *exousía* over a congregation. Considering the volumes and volumes of material written about leadership authority and the submission required, one might reasonably expect there to be a bit more explicit Scripture to the point. The fact that there is not tells us how much inference and assumption has gone into much of what is taught on the subject. There are 346 references in the New Testament to the brotherhood, five references to elders, four to overseers, and one to pastor![36] If you believed what many are writing about the emerging apostles,[37] you might think the emphasis was reversed!

    First, Paul's purpose for authority is explicitly stated in these verses: edification, building up, not ruling over! Second, his tone is again deferring, declining to exercise what had been given him. Paul had authority, but wisely, as in Philemon, defers from using it. We should follow his example.

Summary

The New Testament never normatively uses *exousía*, "to have authority over," to describe relationships between believers or believers and their leaders in a passive way. Authority is something an individual possesses, not a power or privilege someone exercises over another. It is like honor: It can be given or withheld. The power or ability to give or withhold authority belongs to the individual. Others cannot take it or demand it because of function or position. If I give authority to someone, they have *exousía* "over me." If I withhold it, they do not, even if he is a water-walking apostle. The concept of one believer exercising authority over another, or a leader exercising *exousía* over another as the biblical norm, is *alien to the New Testament*. God established authority as necessity in a fallen world to maintain order when love has failed. Love is the norm. Authority is for crisis and in limited spheres of relationship in the church (as we discussed earlier: Paul in his relationships to the disorder in Crete, Corinth, and Thessalonica). We are called to serve one another in love, not rule over one another. Godly authority must have key qualities to be legitimate:

- It must bring life (John 17:2), not just "order."
- It must be empowering (John 1:12; Luke 10:19).
- Its purpose is to more effectively manifest the kingdom (Matthew 10:1; Mark 6:7; Luke 9:1).

CHAPTER 5

SPIRITUAL COVERING: COME OUT, COME OUT, WHEREVER YOU ARE!

Christians often live far below their potential. What we express with our mouths often does not match what we express with our lives: the "profession-expression gap." While our behavior does not save us, it does have kingdom impact. Few things hinder Christ's interests in the lives of unbelievers more effectively than the poor testimony of His own. Our evangelistic efforts can be near impossible because of the debris of bad testimony left by the Christian who may have gone before us. This doesn't excuse the unbeliever, but it sure doesn't make our task easier! It is not a matter of living some sort of idealistic, perfect, or fault-free existence in order to qualify as a bona fide Christian witness. Romans 8:19 says the creation awaits the manifestation of "sons." That is relational. What the world longs to see is *genuineness in relationships*: with God, each other, and the world.

A noble goal pursued by ignoble means becomes an ignoble goal. Perplexed leaders throughout history have attempted to address this profession-expression gap by preaching and teaching various forms of "discipleship" and "accountability." However, the press for discipleship is frequently counterproductive and often disastrous. In the US, approximately 80% of young people raised in the Church will leave by the age of twenty-one and never come back. I would suggest that indicates something is wrong in our goals, mindset, means, and methods. Bad fruit comes from a bad root.

A Bad Idea That Just Won't Go Away

One of the deficient methods used historically[1] to attempt to close this gap, which is experiencing modified and expanded resurgence in the emergent apostolic movement, is the doctrine of "spiritual covering." Those of us over forty are old enough to remember the discipleship movement of the seventies. It was the poster child of good intentions gone bad. To their great and eternal credit, many of the primary leaders of the movement later repented for their error and the excesses of the movement.

There are many degrees and variations on this teaching. At its most benign level, having a spiritual covering is used in a non-technical sense of relating to someone who looks out for or cares for me. Certainly, the lack of genuine care for one another, and especially for pastors and leaders, is epidemic in the church. Most people are in it for themselves. Finding an authentic Christian who genuinely cares for your welfare is a wonderful thing. Caring for one another and looking out for one another is as elemental to Christianity as chicken to the colonel. The problem is twofold: 1) *covering* is not the term the Bible uses for mutual care (the misuse of terminology can get us in trouble), and 2) though benign in intent, it easily becomes malignant in expression.

The doctrine espouses that everyone needs a spiritual covering— someone to whom they are accountable. Allegedly, the divine order is: husbands cover wives, pastors cover their church, apostles cover pastors (and other ministries submitted to them), and other apostles cover apostles. I have found that the last of this list can be pretty weak. Dr. C. Peter Wagner honestly points out that the matter of apostle-to-apostle accountability "is not totally resolved."[2] That is a kind way of putting it.

Authority can be an intoxicating brew. It is far easier to exercise it than yield to it or yield it to another. This is another reason why it is a mistake to define apostles and the apostolic movement primarily in terms of authority, rather than from a center of Calvary-consciousness. Great authority or "visionary leadership" do not distinguish apostles but rather their patience, power, love, and suffering.[3] We will talk more about this in the next chapter.

Spiritual covering doctrine slides from, at best, a poor choice of words[4] for benign care to damnable doctrine when it is: a) defined positionally in terms of position and office, and b) when the one providing the alleged covering becomes a literal broker for divine blessing to flow or spiritual protection to be in place for an individual or church. Some believe that a spiritual covering is a power dimension, a literal spiritual force-field keeping "bad things" from happening to believers and releasing "good things" to the believer[5] It is alleged that individual believers and the church corporately must be under the protective shield of an individual apostle's covering.[6]

What does this doctrine say about: a) Satan's ability to "get at the saints," and b) the Lord's ability to take care of His own? It is not well thought out. It needs to be rejected for the superstitious spiritual paranoia that it is. The power of the life of Christ is in participation with Him in His death and resurrection,[7] not in the spiritual covering of an apostle. Whether or not we have relationship with others who can speak to and care for us is not the issue. It is the implication of the idea that a man, any man, can take the place of Christ: "Who is your spiritual covering?" as defined by rank and positioning. When maintenance of "governmental alignment" or "staying under covering" are contingent for the believer to receive divine blessing or to avoid divine judgment,[8] we have embraced an anti-Christ spirit, regardless of how well intended our motives may be.

It Takes a Village . . .?

Apostolic covering does not answer the primordial question, "Am I my brother's keeper?" The believing community does. Responsibility for one another rests on the corporate community, not a single pastor or apostle. Care is not a leadership duty, nor an apostolic one: it is a believer's task. The fact that care is so rare and falls so frequently on the shoulders of leaders is a sign of our dysfunction, not divine alignment with principle. The problem is leaders illicitly *enjoy* the feeling of having others dependent on them. Lazy and passive believers are only too willing to comply.

In the New Covenant, believers are to:

- discipline one another (1 Corinthians 5:3–5, 6:1–6),
- warn the unruly (1 Thessalonians 5:14),
- admonish one another (Romans 15:14),
- teach one another (Colossians 3:16),
- care for one another (1 Corinthians 12:25),
- exhort one another (Hebrews 3:13, 10:25),
- confess sin to and pray for one another (James 5:16),
- encourage one another (1 Thessalonians 5:11),
- stir up to love and good works (Hebrews 10:24),
- serve one another (Galatians 5:13 and more).

Who says it is the pastor or apostle who must provide all care and counseling functions? To think so is to view ministry from position rather than function, as we talked about in chapter 3 (higher authority). If what you need is a word of knowledge, why go to a pastor who does not operate in that gift, just because he is the pastor? The notion that a given individual (pastor, apostle, whomever) is fully equipped with all resource, for every situation and need, simply because of their positional delegated office, is simply insanity. If you need discernment or prophetic insight, don't go to a pastor whose gifts are compassion and exhortation! Go to where the supply is, regardless of the vessel! If you want gasoline, you don't go to the library to get it! You go to where the resource is! The doctrine of spiritual covering inhibits this because only the "set office," the "set man," the pastor/apostle/leader, is divinely mandated to give approval and sanction to such inquiries. By definition, all inquiry and appeal must be made to him. It is a formula for the eternal infancy of the saints.

I can hear the anxious voice: "Well, what if the person's advice is wrong? What if they make a mistake?" First, advice and counsel should never be given with thus-saith-the-Lord authority (unless dealing with biblically explicit sin issues). It is just advice, one member to another; one member trying to administer the gift of the grace of God in them to another's benefit. We must empower and dignify one another by allowing one another the freedom to take what we may advise to the Lord in prayer and, for better or worse, make our own decisions. If the matter is not one of doctrinal authority, major sin or behavioral issues (legitimate areas of leadership authority, as we have seen), let people grow by making mistakes. Give them the freedom to be wrong, stumble, make errors, and discover Him in the process. The Holy Spirit is surprisingly competent in shepherding His own.

The honest truth is much of what goes for sonship, accountability, and staying "under cover" in the church is based on *two fears*: the fear of *failure* in the subordinates, and the fear of *being hurt* in the leader (pastor, apostle, spiritual father).

Under pressure to close the profession-expression gap, we have cultivated a fear of failure in our congregations. Leaders are afraid that the "sheep" will live carelessly, without holiness, and/or do something wrong bringing reflective disrepute on themselves as leaders. Individual believers are reluctant to minister or act independently[9] because they are afraid they will do it wrong and suffer consequences from leadership or the community because of it.[10] Paul did not look for accountable men, he looked for faithful ones (2 Timothy 2:2).

Think about the logical implications of the covering/set-man doctrine as it is widely practiced. What is the implication if everyone under a leader's care must submit at all times, get approval for all personal decisions, because it is the essence of right governmental alignment to the delegated Ephesians 4:11 office as "the covering head" of the ministry? It requires that the leader functionally proclaim he/she has been divinely endowed to have the insight necessary to meet all needs, at all times, with all wisdom, for all people under his/her care. Since God is the only one who possesses such fullness (and has distributed it in His body, not to the leader), the thinking is delusionally grandiose at best and blasphemous at worst. Dressing it up in the language of "responsibility and care for the people" does not change the fundamental essence: it fosters dependency on the leader in inappropriate ways. A leader's job is to raise others to levels of grace competency so that the resources of Christ are more effectively distributed to the body, through the body, not through the leader.

If we are serious about mutual care one for another rather than delegation to a covering leader, it takes on the feeling of quite a job. Indeed, there is the rub. Americans believe the way to fix a problem is to throw money at it. American believers are the same. The altar of American worship is time, not materialism and consumerism. We would rather pay someone to function for us, because, well, we are just "too busy." We suffer authoritarian abuse by giving illegitimate submission to someone who will make decisions for us, tell us what to do, when and how to do it, guarantee its outcome, and take the blame for failure. Why? I am too busy and can't be bothered. That's what we pay the pastor for and that's why we submit to the covering apostolic father. He will act for me . . . and if things go bad, I can blame him, because, after all, I submitted to my covering, did what he said, it didn't work out, therefore it is not my fault, it is his. This is not just about over-reaching apostolic authority. The doctrine would never get out of harbor if passive and insecure saints were not complicit in the scheme of things—consciously or otherwise.

You can tell someone's true value system, not by where their offerings go, but where his/her time is spent. In a culture of prosperity and abundance like ours, money is no longer the most valued commodity, time is. In a climate where money abounds, it is just too easy to throw money at a problem and think we have "done our bit" for the cause. Ask for time and relational investment and you will get a reaction. We are simply unwilling to make the time investment for New Covenant life to be a reality and have soothed our conscience with the false belief that money will do the job practically; and staying under cover and governmental alignment will do it spiritually.

Leaders who like the attention and authority, and passive saints who like to have it that way, are the life support system of the spiritual-covering doctrine. They form an unholy partnership of silent commitment to keep the whole thing running, though founded on a lie.[11]

The Real Two-Headed Monster

As mentioned in previous chapters, leaders who believe their calling is to execute divine initiative on behalf of the saints, often use the analogy that anything with two heads is a monster. The implication is that being "head" means the executive in charge authorized to provide leadership direction in the church and that cannot be accomplished where there are two executive heads. Well, as I have stated earlier, this is unsound theologically and as an analogy, but let's go with it for a moment. There is a genuine two-headed monster in the church, and it is not aggressive congregants trying to grasp for executive control. It is the emergent apostolic and its emphasis on apostolic authority and staying under covering.

The New Apostolic Priesthood

Our Protestant forefathers gave their life's blood at the stake to do away with the belief system that required a class of religious professionals to broker or mediate the blessings of heaven to the believer. They must be rolling over in their graves. It is beyond painful to see the resurrected form of this doctrine being espoused in apostolic circles and foisted under the banner of "new revelation," "restoring apostolic covering," and "apostolic authority." It is not new revelation. It is old heresy in a new dress.

The notion is put forth by some in the apostolic movement that apostles connect the body to Christ the Head, thereby providing a covering for the body and that without this apostolic connection, the full measure of blessing cannot be realized by the believer, because life and power flow through the apostles to the believer.[12] This is not viewed mystically or spiritually, but rather quite literally, methodologically, and governmentally. Individual apostles allegedly provide divinely designed and necessary protective spiritual covering, and broker divine blessing to individuals "under their covering."[13] Variations of the teaching abound:

> We all need spiritual cover over us—a person or group to give counsel or advice when necessary.[14]

> If we want to remain obedient to God and be blessed, we have but one choice when it comes to delegated authority—submission and obedience.[15]

> A person who has not submitted to the apostolic structure of authority has already violated God's authority chain and that person is now ministering without a spiritual covering of protection.[16]

> Such a violation allows the enemy to come in to the work of the Lord.[17]

> Two major things may happen in the spirit realm when a violation like this takes place. One, the itinerant minister is ministering without any spiritual covering over his life and thereby opening his life and the church he is ministering to for demonic attacks. The other is that the enemy has already gained grounds in the loose structure of that church and with opportunity will find someone to exploit and hold the church at ransom.[18]

Remember: stay under cover![19]

You need the added protection that a solid spiritual covering can bring your life.[20]

God is under no obligation to protect us when we resist his direction but will guard those who are surrendered and in place.[21]

Don't miss this: God's covering is released to us when we are rightly connected in our families and our churches.[22]

When we're positioned in Him and connected to His provision, the canopy of His protection rises high and strong over us.[23]

So in my view, it's far better to stay covered and connected, if we can keep it balanced.[24]

Apostles are like spiritual umbrellas. They cover and protect those under them.[25]

Is it my imagination or is some of this blasphemous? In the New Covenant era, there is no need of a second head to broker, cover, or protect. The Holy Spirit is the Agent who administers the blessing of Christ to individuals, not covering apostles. Don Rumble says it like this:

> The apostolic man who laid the foundation for the local church must not interfere with the headship of Jesus by functioning as "second head" to the work. There is only one head of any expression of Christ's body: Jesus.[26]

> Some have said that the gifts of the Holy Spirit operative in the church are to express the body of Christ, while the leaders (the five-fold ministry, the apostles, etc.) are to reveal the headship of Christ. Such thinking is dangerous. Instead of leaders seeing themselves as simply part of Christ's body, with distinct giftings and responsibilities, they begin to see themselves as uniquely joined to the Head. A basis for clergy/laity distinction is established.[27]

God has sent Him *(the Holy Spirit)* to reveal the Headship of Christ among His people.[28]

After laying the foundation at Corinth, Paul did not commend the church there to the "ministry team of elders" as those representing the head; He entrusted them to Christ.[29] (I might add he did not commend the believers at Corinth to a "covering apostle" either!)

You can tell a church culture has crossed the line of healthy mutual submission in the realm of advice and counsel into an ungodly spiritual covering paradigm when the common interior language of the church or ministry regarding personal decisions is made up of phrases like this:

- "Have you cleared this with the pastor?"
- "Have the elders approved?"
- "What does your apostle have to say about it?"
- "That sounds good, but did you submit it to your covering?"

As we have shown in earlier sections, if it is not a matter of biblical doctrine, major sin, or behavioral issues, the matter is none of the apostle's or pastor's business! If an individual *desires* to receive their input, *fine and dandy!* If they are free to *ignore the input, double fine and dandy!* If they are *required to get it*, or *required to comply with it*, or made to feel like they are coming out from under cover if they do not get pre-approval and yield to it, this is simply a control spirit dressed up in clerical garb, and the line into cultic behavior has been crossed.

Whence Cometh Such Things?

While at least attributing good motive to those who espouse this doctrine, as attempting to close the profession-expression gap, one has to ask, what is the scriptural base for the teaching? The answer: thin . . . lean . . . none.

In the New Testament, there are two words used for *cover* or *covering*: *kalupto* and *peribolaiou*. *Kalupto* is used for the generic sense to cover something. It is *never used* to describe any relationship between believers. *Peribolaiou* is used in one of the most notoriously difficult passages of Scripture (1 Corinthians 11:15) where it is sometimes translated as *veil* and sometimes as *head covering*. In Hebrews 1:12, the King James Version translates it (for better or worse) as *vesture*. The word is not used anywhere else in the New Testament. That is it! Neither word for *cover* or *covering* is used to describe any relationship between any believer and leader. It is simply not there. In his characteristically straightforward fashion, Gordon Fee suggests the following:

> Almost certainly, therefore, by this idiom Paul is referring to an external cloth covering. Beyond that, everything is more speculative.[30]

> We simply have to admit we do not know[31] [what the covering practice was all about].

> We simply do not know what the practice was they were abusing.[32]

> But finally we must beg ignorance. Paul seems to be affirming the "freedom" of women over their own heads; but what that means in this context remains a mystery.[33]

Refreshingly honest.

For our purposes, the key passage is 1 Corinthians 11:16: "If anyone is *philoneikos* (contentious, quarrelsome, wrangler, quarrel lover, disputatious), we have no such custom, neither do the churches of God."

Clearly, the matter was a local issue of custom at Corinth, not a universal principle from which (allowing even the widest berth of inference) a universal spiritual-covering doctrine can be legitimately squeezed out.

Since there is simply no exegetical base in the New Testament for the doctrine of spiritual covering, where do its practitioners get it? Primarily from three sources:

1. Inferentially from the head and headship passages we have already discussed
2. Old Testament typology
3. Unfortunate and careless hymns and choruses concerning the blood of Jesus

Old Covenant Coverings

Coverings everywhere characterize the Old Covenant in stark contrast to the New. A quick reading or word search will make it plain. This is a significant difference between the two covenants. Adam and Eve covered their nakedness, God himself, providing the skin for the task. Coverings and their details take up large portions of text concerning the tabernacle of Moses. The cherubim over the ark of the covenant are the "covering angels." They cover their faces. Moses covered his face after the Sinai encounter, and on and on. The theme is everywhere.

In Genesis 9, the Scriptures record the commendation of Noah's two sons for covering their father's nakedness when he got drunk after the flood. It is completely biblical to speak of covering one another's offenses, weaknesses, sins, etc. It is a manifestation of love to do so: love covers. However, this covering is not a governmental order limited to a few apostolic office holders. It is a body-relational dynamic. We are all supposed to cover one another in this sense, not just leaders over subordinates. It is completely *unbiblical* to speak of covering one's *person* in a *governmental* or *positional* way.

The glory and message of the New Covenant is the absence of coverings! The message of the New Covenant, without exception, is about the removal of veils, coverings, limitations, fears, and mediators.[34] The covering veil of the temple was rent at Calvary! The New Covenant is characterized, not by a covered relationship but an open (*anakalupto*)-

face relationship.[35] In 2 Corinthians 3:14, Paul explicitly contrasts the difference between the two covenants in terms of covering: the Old is covered, the New is not. Our glory in Christ as stated in Hebrews 4:16 is that we might come boldly (*Gr. parrhesia:* outspokenness, frankness, bluntly, publicly, fully assured) to the throne of grace, not hesitantly. The coverings of the Old Covenant were temporary until the coming of Him who would in His person render them unnecessary.

Those who want to teach the doctrine of spiritual or apostolic covering from Old Covenant stories and verses simply do not understand the change in the cosmic order that took place at Calvary/Pentecost. The reestablishment of a governmental order based on covering is not new apostolic revelation, it is regression into the covenant of bondage, and the fruit of the doctrine will be bondage, not safety, blessing, and divine order.[36]

Nice Tune, Bad Theology

The first-century heretic, Arius, got his doctrines established by putting them to catchy melodies and getting the common man to whistle and sing his tunes. His doctrine was absorbed in the mind through the wings of an airy melody. Unfortunately, the same thing happens frequently in the church, especially since the explosion of worship choruses in the last thirty years, which while helpful in terms of singability and beautiful in arrangement, are often not exactly pillars of deep theological thought but rather quite inaccurate.[37]

Nowhere is this truer than our understanding of the blood of Jesus and its relationship to sin. Much of the impetus for the doctrine of spiritual or apostolic covering is absorbed through unfortunate hymns and choruses that emphasize the believer being covered by the blood of Jesus. The connection is made along this line: if the blood of Jesus needs to cover us to protect us from danger and harm, it is not too big a step to believe we need other coverings to protect us from danger and harm, obligingly provided by apostles or other ministers.

Shocking as it may be to some, *there is not a single New Testament verse that says the blood of Jesus covers us.* Blood covering is a *thoroughly Old Covenant concept*; one that is temporary, not permanent. One of the most significant changes from the Old to New Covenant is what was only covered in the Old is washed, purged, cleansed, and utterly removed in the New. Sin that is covered is sin that is still present. Jeopardy exists if the covering is removed. Sin that is washed has been removed. There is no jeopardy, no danger. The pitiable psychological and practical reality is that most Christians live like their sin is covered, not gone. They live their lives in the constant dread of being discovered as not being up to date on their sin, as if some of it was going to leak through the blood covering like ice cream on a dip-top cone on a summer day. They live in perpetual fear of sin leakage and the risk of the punishment it entails.[38]

Even in the Old Covenant era, the psalmist speaks of sins being removed as far as the east is from the west,[39] cast into the sea of divine forgetfulness; not covered, lingering under the surface just waiting for the first error to cause them to be manifest. The psalmist got a peek into the future glories of the New Covenant era. The glory of the New Covenant is that our sins have been removed, not covered.

There is no greater jeopardy than to be confronted with ones sins before a holy God. If Christ has taken care of this dread, not by covering but by washing, from what do believers need protection, and who on earth is going to provide it more than Christ has already done? Apostles? Hardly.

On Account of Being Accountable

Perhaps a reader might be thinking, *Crosby, all we are trying to do is assure responsible and accountable behavior, what is wrong with that?* First, like covering, accountability is an unbiblical term, and in application it can, and often does, exceed biblical grounds. Do a word search (King James Version) sometime on *accountable* or *accountability*. It is not there. We use the term in our language as an attempt to approximate the biblical term *submission.*

Second, as the concept is taught in apostolic circles it is interpreted and practiced as being under someone else and being "accountable to them" in an upstream, individual, and positional way: accountability is to the person "over you," your spiritual covering. The Scriptures teach no such thing.

Issues of accountability are nowhere in Scripture limited to a covering minister or apostle. The burden is *on* each of us, *for* each of us. The responsibility for ministry is with the saints! For all the talk during the last fifty years of "equipping the saints," we have done a fairly poor job, and principles of biblical accountability only exacerbate the situation.

External accountability is like driving with the sheriff in the backseat of your car. As long as the sheriff is there, no one is going to speed! Remove the external presence of authority and a speeder is reborn! Accountability only enables performance-based religion. It is the self-aware, self-monitoring Adamic counterfeit of biblical discipleship. All restraints, codes, and principles of accountability are impotent to change the nature. Accountability can be, and often is, faked. The Adamic nature can comply with the accountability expectations of spiritual covering:

- Have you done your prayers? *Check.*
- Have you read the Word? *Check.*
- Did you do your assignment? *Check.*
- Have you paid your tithe? *Check.*
- Did you pray with your wife? *Check.*
- Did you volunteer at the food bank? *Check.*
- Did you pet the dog today? *Check.*
- *Check . . . check . . . check . . .* , all done sir!

What a good boy or girl you have been!

This so-called "accountability" doesn't touch the realm of death and resurrection life of the Son. It is all about performing tasks to standard. This is not biblical submission or discipleship. It does not produce spiritual maturity. It assures eternal infancy. In fact, it is a stupefying inoculation against Spirit life, because as long as someone has completed their "accountability sheet" for the week, he or she will think they are just spiritually fine when they are the walking dead. They can be relationally a disaster, but if they have submitted their discipleship worksheet on time for the week to their "mentor," or "spiritual covering," they will have the false impression that all is just fine. Accountability is better than unbridled sin, but the manifestation of the life of the Son is superior to policed accountability.

Summary

There is simply not a single New Testament verse to support the doctrine of spiritual or apostolic covering. It is hard to understand how so much has been made based on so little. It must be inferentially supported from other Scriptures. First Timothy 2:5 and Hebrews 12:24 tell us clearly that there is only one mediator between God and man, the One Mediator, Christ Jesus. The notion that a pastor or apostle acts as a mediator to protect, sanctify, or otherwise broker divine blessing to the believer is not new revelation but warmed-over Romanism:

> It is manifest, therefore, that we should look upon the bishop even as we would look upon the Lord Himself, standing as he does, before the Lord.

> For He that is subject to these [bishops and presbyters] is obedient to Christ who has appointed them; but he that is disobedient to these is disobedient to Christ.

> Let us be careful, then, not to set ourselves in opposition to the bishop, in order that we may be subject to God. . . . and that being subject to the bishop and the presbytery, ye may in all respects be sanctified. (St. Ignatius in Epistle of Ignatius to the Ephesians[40])

The doctrine of apostolic covering is super-sized discipleship teaching dressed in the garments of new apostolic insight and the alleged recovery of God's divine governmental order. We have substituted apostles for bishops, networks for denominations, and think we are progressing. It must be called for what it is: baseless fantasy of the ambitions of man.

Jesus is the Head of each local church. Apostles do not hold a hierarchical position of authority over the churches as a mediator between them and God. Their desire is to see local churches founded on Jesus Christ and overseen by a group of elders. Then they can move into new territory in order to see new fellowships of believers established.[41]

PART 3

THE VIEW FROM THREE FEET

CHAPTER 6

FATHERS AND SONS

Behold, I will send you Elijah the prophet before the coming of the great and dreadful day of the LORD: And he shall turn the heart of the fathers to the children, and the heart of the children to their fathers, lest I come and smite the earth with a curse.

—Malachi 4:5-6

I write not these things to shame you, but as my beloved sons I warn *you*. For though ye have ten thousand instructors in Christ, yet *have ye* not many fathers: for in Christ Jesus I have begotten you through the gospel.

—1 Corinthians 4:14-15

Over the last fifteen or twenty years much has been taught and written concerning spiritual fathers and spiritual sons.[1] Teaching within the apostolic renewal regularly refers to apostles as spiritual fathers (as well as other metaphors) and those under their covering as sons. The father-son relationship is allegedly the model from which leaders conduct effective ministry and the way to build local churches according to God's prescribed order. Governmental alignment to a covering apostolic father is presented as the prerequisite to divine blessing and unity under a singular (fathering) head who provides ministry cohesion and direction. It is alleged by many that only a single executive head can provide the necessary unity for corporate purpose and failure at this point is risky:

> Folks, when we mess with God's established order, we miss God's enormous blessings.[2]

Don Rumble points out the spiritual weakness of this view:

> Unity then can only be conceived of as attainable through organizational methods. The key words become "compromise" and "submission." Such an approach to unity requires men to *compromise* in order to find the middle ground that all can stand on, even if it means agreeing to things some consider wrong. It also demands that people submit to the plans of the one(s) in the leading position(s) of the association, Unity then is seen as the accomplishing of stated goals within a peaceful atmosphere.
>
> However, unity in the biblical sense is the revelation of the nature of God through a diverse people (Jn. 17:11, Ephesians 4:16). Organizational methods will never achieve the miracle of "bodyness" (many different people with distinct giftings moving as one under the headship of Christ). Real unity is miraculous and requires the glory of God. (Jn. 17:21–23).[3]

Surely, father-son language and imagery saturates the Scripture. God identifies himself generationally as the God of Abraham, Isaac and Jacob: fathers and sons. God sent a Son. The answer to humanity's need is not a thing, or a how to, or a what, but a who—a Son. In Romans 7, Paul cried out for deliverance, not asking for an explanation or a precept, but a deliverer—a Who. The creation longs and waits, not for an answer, but for whom: sons to be manifest.[4] One of the great glories of the New Covenant is the filial relationship the believer has not just with "God," but with the Father. In His ascension, glorification and Spirit outpouring, Jesus accomplished a cosmic relational change: His Father became ours.[5] Inheritance is an unavoidable theme of Scripture. However, if the devil cannot get us to overtly sin and fail God, he will take God's own beautiful precepts and twist them slightly or push them beyond divine limits, where a God-concept becomes corrupted.

I am afraid this is the case with father-son teaching. The horse of apostolic fathering has been feeling its oats. It does not belong in the glue factory but back in the corral, and bridled, so folks can enjoy the ride without getting thrown off. Broken bodies currently litter the apostolic corral. A scripturally legitimate motif has exceeded divine limits, becoming deceptive, abusive, and corrupt. It must be reigned in. Effective ministry and strong churches are not built by aligning them to spiritual fathers in a new apostolic order of government but by teaching them to plumb the depths of the Person, Christ Jesus: the Sure Foundation.

Call No Man Father

Within apostolic circles it is common to hear language such as:

- "I am one of so and so's spiritual sons."
- "So and so is my spiritual father/mother."
- "He/she is one of my sons/daughters."
- "I provide fatherly covering for my spiritual sons and daughters."
- "My pastor is my spiritual father."
- "I am the apostolic father to my network."

Those who make a practice of using this language and functioning in the relationships related to this language have not given serious consideration to the implications of Matthew 23:8–12 (emphasis mine):

But be not ye called Rabbi: for one is your Master, even Christ; and *all ye are brethren. And call no man your father upon the earth*: for one is your Father, which is in heaven. Neither be ye called masters: for one is your Master, even Christ. But he that is greatest among you shall be your servant. And whosoever shall exalt himself shall be abased; and he that shall humble himself shall be exalted.

Protestants cavalierly dismiss this admonition as having no personal application. The Roman priesthood is too big a target for Protestant arrows to miss. Unfortunately, the Roman speck obscures the Protestant log. The emphasis on honoring leadership[6] and using honor titles[7] in apostolic circles does not take second fiddle to any Roman practice. In spirit, it is not an iota different than any Roman custom, and in practice the level of veneration and honor ascribed to "spiritual fathers" in the apostolic movement would make a cardinal turn redder than his cape with embarrassment. The rational used for honor titles is "it teaches the people honor and respect." Maybe, maybe not.

There is nothing wrong with giving honor to whom honor is due as long as it is in a *community of mutuality*, where the *least honorable are given the greater honor*![8] We are to honor every one,[9] not just the pastor of the church or the apostle of the network. In thirty years of church experience in various local church environments and diverse theological backgrounds, I received copious teaching on 1 Timothy 5:17 (giving double honor to leaders: e.g. pastors, apostles, etc.). Yet, at the same time, I have never heard a single practical message preached on 1 Corinthians 12:23–25 (honoring the least honorable), nor seen regular policies and protocols of honor implemented to emphasize those verses with the same sense of conviction with which honor of leaders is preached.

I would like to put out a simple challenge to the church leader who might be irritated with me while reading this: Who gets the best seating in your church? Who gets the best parking space? Who gets special days of appreciation in their honor? Who has the finest office? Who has access to the VIP snack room after service? The dear saint who quietly takes care of his/her invalid mother everyday without fanfare? Or the glow-in-the dark apostle/bishop who is in for a weekend's worth of meetings? Uh, Houston . . . we have a problem. When honor flows in one direction—upstream—to hierarchy, position, ministry, office, and rank, we are on ungodly ground, even with 1 Timothy 5:17 hanging on our lips.

The Matthew 23:8–12 passage is clearly a divine ban. The King James Version *ye* in verse 8 is emphatic.[10] In modern street English, it could be rendered: *"Listen up, I am talking to you . . . this means you!"* The implication of these verses goes beyond a generic ban on using inflated titles of honor, or false prestige, though these are undoubtedly included. Jesus specifically mentions three distinct classes, or categories, in His ban: Rabbi, father, and master. Why would the Lord mention these three? What would these titles or terms have in common, beyond being generally honorific, that the Lord would so group them? We need to understand some cultural background.

Rabbi

A full examination of the role of the rabbis in first-century Judaism is beyond the scope of this writing. However, one element has bearing on this topic. The rabbis believed that, as teachers of Torah to the people, they were the guides into, or the brokers of, eternal life to Israel.[11] They believed they had power, through their teaching of the Torah, to give or withhold access to eternity. Christ refers to this in verse 13 when He describes the Pharisees and scribes "shutting up heaven" to their followers. *Abba*[12] (father) was also a term applied to and desired by the rabbis. In their culture, leading or guiding someone made you metaphorically their master; hence, Jesus uses the term almost synonymously with rabbi.

Father

Naturally speaking, a father is someone without whom you would not have literal, physical existence. A father is responsible (with obvious partnering help!), not for bringing life to you, but in a sense, bringing you to life. He is the agent, or broker, of your physical existence. Without him (parents), you could not experience physical life.

Master

First-century Palestine was a patronage culture, not an individual merit culture. To advance in society, or at times to even have access to the essentials of life, it was necessary to develop relationship with a rich patron who could assure you of access to monetary resources, or favor. You could not categorically advance in their society through hard work and self-effort. That is a thoroughly Western, primarily American, value (one of our better ones, though not without weaknesses!). This notion simply did not exist in their culture. You got ahead in life by honor status at birth or by the community granting you honor, not by your own personal merits. In exchange for a patron's favor, the beneficiary was responsible to extol the patron's virtues in the community. The recipient of the patron's favor would often walk behind the patron in public, vocally expressing how wonderful the patron was.[13] Without a sponsoring patron (who would in effect be one's master), the basics of life sustenance often were not accessible. The patron/master was literally responsible for life or death.

What do these three categories have in common and how does it relate to our topic? The members of each group were (literally, figuratively, or spiritually) *brokers of life*. Jesus forbids, not only the use of honorific titles, but at a deeper level, He is saying there is only one life-broker: God/Christ. The modern English word "lord" derives from the old English word "*hlafweard*" meaning, "he who guards the loaf." For millennia, bread has been considered the staff of life. The ancients understood that he who guarded the loaf, was responsible for your life, and was therefore, your *hlafweard* or "lord."

In a kingdom context, there is only one life-brokering Lord, and it is not a covering apostle! We are all equal brethren before the only true Life-broker and Grantor of favor. The only broker of life and blessing to the believer is Christ Himself, *not* a covering spiritual father or apostle. We can all receive blessing from one another, through the diverse giftings and ministries distributed in the body. However, limiting the power to bless to a vested individual in a certain office, or viewing spiritual fathering in a covering and life-brokering capacity is error.

Sons of the Son

Some teach that the prototype model for the relationship between pastor and congregant or apostle and subordinate ministry is the spiritual father-son paradigm. An individual's status as a "spiritual son in the house," or lack thereof, often determines access to spiritual development, training, church membership, promotion or release into personal ministry.

I know of situations where ministry or departmental leadership opportunities were denied to individuals because in the leader's eyes they were not "spiritual sons," supposedly not possessing the pastor's heart as a son and therefore not trustworthy. This was especially painful, as over years and decades the people had demonstrated their love and care for the pastor by their loyalty, finances, and service. However, because of a subjectively perceived lack of a nebulous quality of "spiritual sonship," the individuals were marginalized and neutralized for kingdom expression.

This type of situation reverses the Ephesian 4 mandate. The pastor no longer equips the saints for the work of ministry but disqualifies the saints because they do not facilitate the pastor's ministry—the "vision of the house!" The believer's status in relationship to the pastor/apostle becomes the determinative factor as to whether or not he or she is equipped and released into ministry. It was all done with a deeply-set conviction of conformity to God's Word and "present truth," "new-order revelation and understanding." It is sad and it is abuse.

Much sonship teaching requires spiritual sons to prove their loyalty before being released into their own ministry with the father's blessing and leadership sanction. The teaching allegedly models Luke 16:1-13[14] (serving another person's ministry/vision before God gives you your own) and is typically presented as a concern for the ultimate spiritual success of the sons. In reality it is often an attempt by well-meaning but ignorant and insecure spiritual fathers to avoid being hurt by betrayal.

If a spiritual father is solely surrounded by well-behaved and loyal spiritual sons, he will never experience betrayal or hurt. He will also never experience the life transforming power of the Cross, nor the power of His death and resurrection. Betrayal is as much a part of our faith as anything. Leaders who unconsciously set up authority structures and father-son ministry paradigms as insulation from personal hurt, are actually working contrary to Christ and His purposes in the earth. The sad part is, it can all look so good, sound so biblical, and so "cutting edge." It can also be completely unrecognized by the leader.

The self-preserving Adamic nature will use the biblical motif of sonship to protect itself in those who have unknowingly drifted from a Calvary foundation of ministry through the preaching of topical themes instead of Christ and Him crucified. In so doing, both the minister and the message of sonship are discredited. The reason you don't see the fruit we would expect and desire from the "sonship message" in spiritual sons (and daughters) is because the fathers have not proven their love to such a degree that the sons are willing to lay down their own agendas.[15] If we really believe Malachi 4:5-6, and if fatherhood and maturity carries with it the responsibility of initiative and burden bearing, the issue of the hour is not: "How can we birth spiritual sons and get them under our covering in submissive obedience, but rather, how do fathers fully experience His death and resurrection and become as irresistible as Christ was?" The onus is on the *fathers*, *not* the sons.

Simply because you have been around longer, have more knowledge, and more ministries "under your covering" than others, does not make someone a spiritual father. Spiritual fatherhood is defined by the degree someone has embraced His death and resurrection, not by ministerial "success." Spiritual fathers and leaders who protect themselves, their ministries, pulpits, legacies, inheritance, assets, reputations, churches, networks, salaries, egos, image, platform, presence, and notoriety have no right to call themselves spiritual fathers simply because of kingdom tenure. Their ethics and behavior prove they are not. Because they are not fathers, they also have no right to require their sons to submit to them and abandon their agendas to first "serve another man's vision." The concept of sonship *may be* biblically legitimate to some degree (see below), but our current methods are not. If the big dog never shuts up, the little dog never learns to bark.

WWJD?[16] Jesus volitionally chose a devil[17] to be on his team and did not deny him any access to Himself or opportunity for ministry because he "wasn't a son" and "didn't share his heart." Judas bore the responsibility of his own behaviors and Jesus bore the pain of it. That is what a spiritual father who is not afraid of death and resurrection does. The rest are just insecure posers. Anxiety and fear-based submission and covering schemes will never close the profession-expression gap. They will never produce the quality of sonship in the earth the Lord desires and the fathers long for. This impasse, this broken methodology, this gap, will be closed only by all parties returning to and experiencing Christ and His cross in death and resurrection power.

How legitimate is the concept of "spiritual sonship"? Does it have any limits or boundaries? The Scriptures refer to believers in churches as "children" in several passages such as: 2 Corinthians 6:13, 12:14; 1 Thessalonians 2:7, 2:11; Galatians 4:19; 1 Peter 1:14, and multiple times in John's epistles. The Corinthian and Galatian passages use it as a metaphor for their state of spiritual infancy and not as a compliment! The Thessalonian verses also use the term as a metaphor describing Paul's tenderness and affections among them. First Peter 1:14–15 uses it again as a metaphor for the believer's relationship to *God*, not their leaders or a covering apostle. In John's epistles, it is again a metaphor describing John's affection/heart state toward them, especially in their spiritual infancy.

It is illegitimate to use verses describing affection with limited metaphors to establish an eternal order of relationship, a doctrine of spiritual covering. While a metaphor by definition is an approximation of reality, the *true* reality is that these verses say *nothing* about governmental order in the church. They merely describe an affective state, a heart condition, not hierarchy or subordinancy of position or dependence on an apostle to provide spiritual covering. In the Pauline examples in Galatia and Corinthians, the language is particularly linked to their spiritual infancy, immaturity, and inability to be spiritually discerning in matters of core gospel doctrine and moral behavior! By definition, a *transitory metaphor* we hope to outgrow!

It is appropriate to be dependent in spiritual infancy. It is inappropriate to press this language as justification for a doctrine of eternal subordinancy or covering for the rest of one's life! Even nature itself recoils at such a concept. The little chick grows up, comes out from Momma's covering, and flies, facing the uncertainties and risks of life. The covering doctrine flatters leaders into thinking they are more important and necessary than they are.[18] It is inherently ego gratifying to think that for the rest of an individual's mortal existence I am responsible for his/her spiritual well being. Even though the individual may be fifty years old and a believer for thirty years, it is a requirement of "God's order" that they submit their major life decisions to "me," their covering apostle.

The argument could be made that Paul uses the term *son* to describe his ministry and relationships; therefore, shouldn't we? Paul explicitly refers to *only three people* as his sons: Onesimus, Timothy, and Philemon.[19] He refers to himself as a father in 1 Corinthians 4. Peter refers to Mark as his son *once* in 1 Peter 5:13.

What of Apollos, Silas, Mark, Demas, Aristarchus, Luke, Stephanas, and others? Paul *never* refers to them as his sons. Yet he was clearly in relationship with them, effectively working with them, referring to them as fellow prisoners, helpers, and laborers in the gospel. Sometimes the relationship was as peers and sometimes not. Were they on the disqualified B team because of lack of a "sonship" relationship to Paul? Were they under suspicion from leadership because they were not part of the "house vision?" Of course not.

If we wanted to be "strictly biblical" in our thinking and methods, one has to question the legitimacy of the father-son ministry paradigm for any relationship other than those of a convert and the one who leads him to conversion and subsequent growth in the faith. The apostles reserved the term specifically to those relationships. Some believe the metaphor does not relate to conversion but to being fathered into ministry.[20] There is no indication that Scripture uses the relational metaphor in any other way than conversion. To categorically adopt and adapt the imagery to an American local church full of people with whom the pastor had no role in conversion but who transferred in from another church is a very dubious application of Scripture. It is even more dubious to apply it to a covering apostle who has no relationship with an individual's conversion or growth but who merely "joined the apostle's network." If fathering is not one-on-one and relational, it does not exist. A spiritual father is not an office one holds due to tenure and rank. It is a quality one possesses and manifests only in relationship.

Father-son terminology is a legitimate, but *limited* biblical *metaphor* describing a precious interpersonal *relationship*, that is born of the Spirit. It is not an *institution of ministerial protocol* that must be adhered to at all costs that can be shopped for like buying a pair of shoes.[21] It is a quality of relationship, not a limiting format for ministry. The problem develops when we try to institutionalize, codify, and reproduce an essentially spiritual quality.

For example, if someone has a genuine, Spirit-birthed relationship with a "spiritual father/mother" and he or she should pass away, is the son or daughter in that relationship now suddenly "out from under covering" and required to "shop for a replacement" because he or she is out of divine order? This is of course an absurd idea that confuses that which is precious and Spirit-wrought with that which is institutional and methodological. You cannot replace a metaphor. You can (and should) establish new relationships of mutual trust and mutual care with others, as we all need someone to care for us—pastor us. Over time a new relationship may deepen and take on new dimensions. However, you cannot replace a bona fide spiritual father-son relationship. There are no stepchildren in the kingdom.

The notion that extending trust only to those whom the leader considers his spiritual sons and daughters is also outside the boundary of a limited biblical metaphor of relationship. The use of the term in such a way classifies and marginalizes people in ungodly categories. The mandate to the Ephesians 4 ministers is to equip the saints for the work of ministry—period, not make sure they maintain "sonship" relationship to the equipper. The equipper's effectiveness with individuals will vary based on degree of heart access allowed by the one being equipped, but this does not legitimize categorizing people.

The logical outcome of much sonship teaching (as commonly taught and practiced) is attractive because it cunningly becomes a new gospel with the leader at the center. The emphasis becomes right relationship to the leader, not right relationship to Christ. At its core, it is a usurping doctrine. It usurps the place, prominence, and uniqueness of Christ. Any "gospel" message with a new center must be called for what it is: anti-Christ. My many friends (who may not be so after they read this!) who are strong advocates of the sonship model will likely strongly disagree. But as Shakespeare said: "The lady doth protest too much methinks."[22] Again, and again, I have seen the phenomenon of a subtle new gospel materialize in circles where the sonship message is preached in preference, emphasis, and frequency over Christ and Him crucified. It is inevitable and as blinding as it is inevitable. When a fish swims in the environment of its waters, it unavoidably absorbs the unknown and unrecognized contaminants in the water. It cannot be helped. The reality is defined by the nature of the environment.

Ephesians 4: 11-13 Governmental Ministries?

And he gave some, apostles; and some, prophets; and some, evangelists; and some, pastors and teachers; For the perfecting of the saints, for the work of the ministry, for the edifying of the body of Christ: Till we all come in the unity of the faith, and of the knowledge of the Son of God, unto a perfect man, unto the measure of the stature of the fulness of Christ: That we henceforth be no more children, tossed to and fro, and carried about with every wind of doctrine, by the sleight of men, and cunning craftiness, whereby they lie in wait to deceive; But speaking the truth in love, may grow up into him in all things, which is the head, even Christ: From whom the whole body fitly joined together and compacted by that which every joint supplieth, according to the effectual working in the measure of every part, maketh increase of the body unto the edifying of itself in love.

(Ephesians 4:11–16)

The relationship of pastor to members is not one of equality, but one of authority. The pastor rules the members just as a shepherd rules over his sheep, a father over his children, and a king over his citizens.

(A quote from a mid-western church's bylaws)

The above quote while perhaps rare in its candor is not rare in sentiment. It is normative of how many in the apostolic movement view the order of God's government and how the pastor/congregation and apostle/network relationship supposedly should look in terms of executive authority.[23] The ethos has dominated my thirty-year experience in the church under the strong set-man style of leadership (more on this in the next section). It contributes to the ungodly clergy-laity gap and to reliance on a class of professional clergy that is at the root of Western church dysfunction. I have personally heard this specific metaphor taught by multiple leaders in different theological and leadership settings. Some tone down the king-citizen metaphor to a version slightly more appealing to American egalitarian politics: president-citizens.[24] This still doesn't paint the barn. It is however typical of how common it is to view the Ephesians 4 ministries from an authority paradigm of government and to make blessings contingent on government and order rather than death and life.

Let's look at the Ephesians 4 passage closely for a moment. Where does the emphasis on government and authority come from? What is it based on? What is the purpose of these ascension gift ministries?

For

The Greek preposition (*pros*) indicates direction, as arriving at an "ultimate purpose." The ultimate purpose of an Ephesians 4:11 minister is not to be the vision caster or the vision setter. It is not about the set man "getting the vision" and requiring the "sons and daughters" to embrace it. That is nothing but American management and success strategy principles washing into the church. Rather, the ultimate purpose of an Ephesians 4 minister follows:

1. **Equipping.** The Greek word is *katartismós*. The New Testament uses it only here. It literally means "mending, repair, setting a bone, refitting a ship, correcting all that is deficient." The calling and vision of an Ephesians 4 minister is to bring healing and wholeness to the Body through all the graces of Christ so the individual believers in the body may be "outfitted" or rigged for effective kingdom function. Listening to some apostles preach you would think the roles are reversed: that the role of the saints is to serve and fulfill the set man's vision!

2. **Saints and the work of ministry.** The term *saints* simply means "separated ones, those who have been separated by the Lord for His purposes" to do, literally, the "labor of service—ministry."[25]

3. **Edified.** This is the Greek *oikodomē*, literally meaning, "to build up." It is an architectural term. It means "to add form and structure," and by inference, "to beautify." By properly outfitting the saints and getting them functioning, form and structure result. The Ephesians 4 minister is not responsible for controlling structure. *Functioning saints are the structure!* Yes, Ephesians 4 ministers, particularly prophets and apostles, are normally concerned about order and structure. But the essence of ministry is not coming up with "my apostolic structure" and having people adorn it like ornaments on a Christmas tree, bringing their lives and resources to support "the dream God has given me." Rather,

it is where I give my life for the interior structure of Christ in the individual, so that the Body is seamlessly built by the increase of Christ, not the increase of structure and government. The people are the dream. There is no other legitimate dream for the Ephesians 4 minister. God cares about people, not dreams and destiny. Dreams and destiny are the vehicle to serve people. When the vehicle becomes the purpose, we are on an ungodly track.

The Inmates are Running the Asylum!

Christ is Lord of a kingdom, not a democracy. Teachers frequently emphasize that because it is a kingdom His delegated and anointed representatives have authority, the people do not. As I said in chapter 2, this is a false, two-dimensional proposition. It is also fortuitously convenient for those teaching it. This is a thoroughly Old Covenant model of understanding. There is a paranoid fear that any movement in governmental structures toward empowering and serving people is a capitulation to democratic-, congregational- committee-operated churches! While not everyone might be as frankly candid with their methods as the quote above (from the church bylaws), the spirit of it pervades leadership circles in the church.

In leadership meetings I have attended, I have heard the people of God referred to in the most demeaning terms such as carnal, broke, poverty mindset, blind, not anointed, spiritually ignorant, "dumb as sheep," lacking discernment, lacking intelligence, etc. (P.S. these are not exaggerations! I have witnessed them all—frequently, commonly, and to my shame, agreed with them and said some myself.) I have sat in numerous executive meetings where the people are viewed with the respect you would give a dog. No, that is too positive: at least you pet a dog. Old Covenant stories such as Moses and the golden calf reinforce this leader-people gap: "Shucks, without us, they will get in all kinds of trouble!" We have shown earlier the inadequacy of these Old Covenant accounts for the basis of New Covenant leadership models.

How foreign these leadership mindsets are to a Pauline spirit! Consider the following Scriptures and remember that a good number of them were written to people in rebellion and on the verge of apostasy!

- Galatians 5:10: "I have *confidence* in you through the Lord, that ye will be none otherwise minded: but he that troubleth you shall bear his judgment, whosoever he be."
- 2 Thessalonians 3:4: "And we have *confidence* in the Lord touching you, that ye both do and will do the things which we command you."
- 2 Corinthians 2:3: "And I wrote this same unto you, lest, when I came, I should have sorrow from them of whom I ought to rejoice; having *confidence* in you all, that my joy is the joy of you all."
- 2 Corinthians 7:16: "I rejoice therefore that I have *confidence* in you in all things."
- 2 Corinthians 8:22: "And we have sent with them our brother, whom we have oftentimes proved diligent in many things, but now much more diligent, upon the great *confidence* which I have in you."
- Romans 15:14: "And I myself also am *persuaded* of you, my brethren, that ye also are full of goodness, filled with all knowledge, able also to admonish one another."
- Philemon 1:21: "Having *confidence* in thy obedience I wrote unto thee, knowing that thou wilt also do more than I say."
- Philippians 1:6: "Being *confident* of this very thing, that he which hath begun a good work in you will perform *it* until the day of Jesus Christ. . . ."
- Hebrews 6:9: "But, beloved, we are *persuaded* better things of you, and things that accompany salvation, though we thus speak."[26]

These apostolic remarks were written *to the people*, not the church leadership, not the elder board, not the covering apostle. Some might say that the apostles, primarily Paul, wrote in "prophetic hope," not actual reality; and that the people were not really trustworthy, but in writing so positively about them, he was trying to draw out the quality for which he was hoping for. I would offer that Paul actually believed the Holy Spirit was in the people of God, even among the babes, the weak, the carnal, and the struggling.

I would ask, as leaders, who do we think we are? When a leader loses his or her scope as being a servant *to* the flock, while they are one *of* the flock,[27] and instead assumes a posture of being *above or over* the flock, as having in their leadership call some sort of innate quality that sets them apart in a special privileged class of illumination, we are in a most grievous place indeed.

A peril in some churches is the exaltation of ministers above the level of humanity, the centering of churches in the person and authority of the clergy.[28]

The mark of genuine apostles, or any church leader, is not how much authority they wield, nor loyalty and submission they require, but how much they defer to Christ. I am not advocating abdication of executive authority into the hand of the lowest common denominator among the masses—the paralyzing fear in every set man. I am passionate for a change in *theology, tone, methods,* and *spirit.*

Ephesians 4:11–13 *says nothing about government.* Ephesians 2:20 says apostles and prophets are foundational, not governmental. They do not rule over the body, sitting as the chief executive; they are under the body, providing the hidden strength and substructure. The purpose of the Ephesians 4 ministries is quite explicit: for the perfecting of the saints for the work of ministry. They are establishing servant ministries, not governmental. They serve both the local church and the Universal Church, but they do not "govern." The King James Version never uses the word *government* associated with any of the five-fold ministries. I believe the Scriptures are precise, and when they are precisely silent, we ought to be too! The idea that these ministries, especially, apostles, are governmental is *assumptive and inferential* from other Scriptures regarding headship and ruling that we have already discussed.

Apostolic Attributes

Many have well documented the basic elements of what constitutes an apostle or the elements of apostolic function.[29] The problem is the emphasis on authority as the distinguishing or primary mark.[30] Describing *what is* as if it were what *should be*, rather than going to the Scriptures, is the error of many diagnosing the current apostolic renewal.[31] Because authority is a dominant feature of the emerging apostolic (I do not challenge that—it is unfortunately true) does not mean it should be.

The first and foremost function of an apostle as a "sent one" is to accurately represent the One who sent him.[32] The emphasis in genuine apostolic ministry is not to see to it that apostles are restored to their proper place as it is to see that *Jesus is restored to His*.[33] Much emphasis in the apostolic movement is how the people under the apostle need to maintain right relationship to their spiritually covering apostle rather than right relationship to *God*!

The job of an apostle is not to preach the restoration of apostles, or covenant, or governmental alignment, or spiritual fathering. The goal of an apostle is to preach Christ and Him crucified and to assure an accurate representation of Christ on earth. The goal of an apostle is not to build his network but to assure that the "building" of God is laid on the Sure Foundation,[34] which is not the governmental order of covering apostles!

In what could be broadly called the "restorationist movement,"[35] there is great talk about the apostles and prophets being restored to their proper place and function. While I loosely agree with that, it is a potentially dizzying idea. There is no shortage of pride in the idea that God's whole show has been deficient for oh, two thousand years, and has been held up waiting for, well, *us*! How *did* the church survive without us!? The much talked about reformation and restoration is *not* about the restoration of certain offices, governments, truths, and ministries to God's people. It is the restoration of *God's Son to His rightful place in our midst*.[36] Some in the apostolic movement have lost this center. They believe the restoration of apostles to their place and position determines whether or not there will be an "end-time harvest." For them, the determining factor is not the manifestation of Christ but the manifestation of apostles. When the apostles begin to arise by the thousands, we will be able to take the nations for Jesus Christ. The harvest cannot be brought apart from this foundational office.[37] Happily, there are *some* voices of sanity being raised at the present hour pointing out that the apostolic movement is not about the apostles! It is about an emerging quality in the nature of the church, the corporate man: being more completely conformed to a fully accurate image of Christ.

John Calvin sums up my concern in a typically brilliant way. If the present-day apostles would heed Calvin's advice (not his practice, unfortunately), this book would not be necessary. I am not arguing for the elimination of apostles but their restraint! Calvin's thoughts are worth including at length. (Emphasis is added.)

Now the only way to build up the church is for the ministers themselves to *endeavor to preserve Christ's authority for himself;* this can be secured only if what he has received from his Father be left to him, namely, that he alone is the schoolmaster of the church. For it is written not of any other but him alone, "Hear Him" [Matthew 17:5].

Ecclesiastical power, therefore, is not to be mischievously adorned, but is to be *confined within certain limits,* so as not to be drawn hither and thither at the caprice of men. For this purpose, it will be of great use to observe how it is described by Prophets and Apostles. For if we concede unreservedly to men all the power which *they think proper to assume,* it is easy to see how soon it will *degenerate into a tyranny* which is altogether alien from the Church of Christ.

Therefore, it is here necessary to remember, that *whatever authority and dignity the Holy Spirit in Scripture confers on priests, or prophets, or apostles, or successors of apostles, is wholly given not to men* themselves, but to the ministry to which they are appointed; or, to speak more plainly, to the word, to the ministry of which they are appointed. For were we to go over the whole in order, we should find that they *were not invested with authority* to teach or give responses, *save in the name and word of the Lord.*

With good cause, therefore, the Father appointed the Son our teacher, with special prerogative, commanding that *he and no human being should be heard.* When he said, "Hear him" (Matthew 17:5), he commended his office to us, in few words, indeed, but words of more weight and energy than is commonly supposed, for it is just as if he had withdrawn us from all doctrines of man, and *confined us to him alone,* ordering us to seek the whole doctrine of salvation *from him alone, to depend on him alone, and cleave to him alone; in short (as the words express), to listen only to his voice.*

Hence also we infer that *nothing else was permitted to the apostles* than was formerly permitted to the prophets, namely, *to expound the ancient Scriptures, and show that the things there delivered are fulfilled in Christ.* [38]

Truly there is nothing new under the sun. As poignantly clear and Christ-centered as these quotes are, Calvin's later extreme authoritarianism, only serves to make my point. In spite of writing the above, he became one of the worst authoritarians who ever lived. While railing against the evil authoritarianism in the Roman papacy, he became like them, to the point of executing dissenters. Being able to teach it and being able to live it are two different matters. Revelation is nothing. Life is everything. Authority is intoxicating. Even for the most conscientious, well-meaning, and servant-spirited person, it is two-hundred-proof hooch. Our American forefathers knew it, and the Holy Spirit knows it. Contrary to the emphasis in the emergent apostolic, that apostles need to be vested with authority, they need to be restrained. Unrestrained authority took down John Calvin, and it will take down the apostolic movement and those apostles in it.

Are Not Apostles Set First?

And God hath set some in the church, first apostles, secondarily prophets, thirdly teachers, after that miracles, then gifts of healings, helps, governments, diversities of tongues.

(1 Corinthians 12:28)

For I think that God hath set forth us the apostles last, as it were appointed to death: for we are made a spectacle unto the world, and to
angels, and to men.

> (1 Corinthians 4:9)

We are fools for Christ's sake, but ye are wise in Christ; we are weak,
but ye are strong; ye are honorable, but we are despised.

> (1 Corinthians 4:10)

Does not the Scripture clearly teach that apostles are "set" "first?"
That is what it says. But what does it mean? The word *set* means simply
"to place." An apostle is not "set" in any unique way any more than
any of the other gifts listed. The context of the passage and chapter is
the diversity of God's distribution with each member divinely set in his
or her unique place. Every member is "set" in the body, including the
other ministries listed in verse 12:28.

The word *first* is the Greek word *proton*. It means "first in sequence,
time, or place." Thayer includes first in rank and importance. See, there
it is! Apostles have rank; they are first. Not so fast. This is one of the
situations where word definition is not enough to determine meaning
accuracy, but word usage is just as important. How does the Scripture
use this word in other verses? Sixty verses in the King James Version
use the word. In *fifty-nine* of the sixty verses it is translated "*first in time
or sequence, not rank or position.*" That only leaves *one* other verse. You
guessed it: 1 Corinthians 12:28.

The context of the verse has nothing to do with governmental
authority structures. The apostle is talking about gift distribution in
the church and their function, not hierarchical rank! The monarchial
bias of the King James Version translators shines through again! At the
very least, this should make us slow to make bold, doctrinally-binding
pronouncements of authority concerning apostolic prominence based
on one verse out of sixty! It might even move us to abandon the proposition all together!

This is nothing but bias reading authority and rank into the verse because of our predisposition to see it there. Let's just be consistent. The context is a logical sequence of order in building a church, not first in rank and importance.[39] Apostles are only "first" in importance because without the first foundation the building does not go up. They are first in a building sense but at the bottom in a hierarchical sense.

In describing the work of Geoffrey Bull, Don Milam says:

"Bull's words and work are a model for all who could call themselves apostles in these days. You will not find an emphasis on creating apostolic networks. You will see no hint of pyramid control and subjugation. You will find a man who has experienced Christ in a profound and deeply meaningful way and whose only agenda is to share it with others."[40]

Yes, apostles by reason of their calling are first:

- They were the first to be entrusted with the gospel
- They are first into an area to lay the foundation
- They are the first to impart Christ-centered doctrine
- They are first in responsibility before God
- They are first to lay down their lives
- They are first to suffer
- They are the first to sacrifice
- They are first to be forgotten
- They are first to be misunderstood
- They are last in the eyes of the world and church!

CHAPTER 7

WHO YA GONNA CALL? "MYTH BUSTERS"

Moving the Set Man's Seat

One of the prevalent doctrines in emerging apostolic and restorationist churches (but not limited to them) is the doctrine of the "set man:"

> ...there are no Scriptural grounds for a (sic) autocratic ministry or monarchial bishop, there is scriptural ground for the "set man."
>
> Therefore it is recognized that each congregation must have a set man.
>
> The set man must have vision and direction.
>
> It does appear that any government was always in conjunction with a "first among equals" ministry.[1]

The author of the above, and myriad others, believe that each local church or apostolic network must have not only a team of elders, but from within this team, a senior elder, the alleged "first among equals," the "set man." The set man is the chief executive and visionary of the church or network. At the local church level, it is assumed this is the pastor (senior pastor) and at a network level it is the apostle (senior apostle). The alleged logic behind this thinking is that you cannot lead a family, a church, or network unless there is a singular executive "head" responsible for the "house vision" and overall direction of the fellowship. That is likely true if a leader is defined as the chief visionary responsible for movement, rather than the chief servant responsible for equipping.

Let's examine the set-man doctrine from a biblical basis.

1. The Scriptures never use the term. Isn't it interesting the number of times, in this text, I have had to say this concerning the alleged divine order of God's government as it is commonly taught? In and of itself, that it is no big deal: the Trinity is never "specifically" mentioned either. However, the cumulative effect, I think, is significant. At the very least, skepticism rather than dogmatism is appropriate.

2. The author above admits there is no scriptural basis for monarchial ministry. Monarch means "one ruler: one ultimate and final authority." Changing nouns doesn't fix the problem. Changing from bishop to set man merely shifts the matter from the left to right hand. There is not a lick of difference in substance. The appeal to the "plurality of elders" and "a team" is a sop thrown out to try to fog the obvious. A king or president has counselors and advisors on his team. However, he is still the king.[2] Now, a king can be pleasant and inclusive or harsh and authoritarian. This is all style. In the end, he rules. It is the same in the set-man dogma and practice. In the final analysis, the set-man doctrine is monarchial: one man rules.

3. The author does not provide any New Testament exegesis[3] to support his contention but supports his proposition with Old Covenant verses. We dealt with this line of thinking earlier.

4. The only New Testament verse the author offers to support his conviction (there is no exegesis, just an offering of this verse) is from the letters to the seven churches in Asia in the book of

Revelation. The letters were written to the "angelos" (Gr. *aggelos*), or the messenger, of each local church, whom, without a shred of exegetical support, the author declares to be the set man.

That's It

As Porky Pig would say, "Th, th, th, th, that's all folks!" The entire system of government ardently adhered to and presented as God's order is based on no more than this. Even if the arguments presented were accurate, the sparseness of New Testament evidence should make us view the proposition with strong reservation. Though I believe the doctrine is unsound, even if it were true, one would expect the tone of presentation might be muted in restorationist and apostolic circles because of the lack of clear evidence: "this could be," "this may be," "we think it is so." That is not the case. This author has heard this doctrine espoused for decades as the final, authoritative word concerning God's governmental order. If any should even question the matter, he or she will be accused of being under a spirit of independence, unsubmissive, anti-authority, and so on.[4]

What about the *aggelos*? At best, the set man interpretation is an inference. There are those who are equally convinced the *aggelos* is a literal angel, assigned to watch over the churches. Besides, compare this *single* example to the bulk of the New Testament written (addressed) *to the people*, the churches, the corporate man, not to the alleged set man-*aggelos*, as even the book of Revelation itself was (Revelation 1:4)!

- Galatians 1:1-2
- 1 Thessalonians 1:1
- 2 Thessalonians 1:2
- 1 Corinthians 1:1-2
- 2 Corinthians 1:1
- Romans 1:1, 7
- Colossians 1:1-2
- Ephesians 1:1.
- Philippians 1:1

In all of these letters, except Ephesians, the church was in crisis. Yet Paul addressed none of them to the elders or the set man.[5] Now I know comparative word counts and usage are a poor basis for binding doctrine, but we should at least compare emphasis: one passage of dubious inference compared to the bulk of the Pauline letters. Where is the scriptural emphasis?[6]

The set-man doctrine is an exegetically threadbare beggar. It is unsound and not something upon which we should base a jot of binding doctrine requiring churches and individuals to conform their lives to as if it was God's divine order. At best, it is a weak inference; and at worst, out and out error. My compass leans strongly toward the latter.

First Among Equals and Rank

As has been common throughout our discussion (covering, government, etc.), the Scriptures never use the phrase, "first among equals." Here again, we see a biblically unsustainable concept put forward as a binding precept for conformity to alleged order and structure. It is an inference. It is terminology used to legitimize what we think the Scripture says. Again, that in itself is not a terminal problem. There are lots of legitimate things that the Scripture does not explicitly mention. However, when a lot is made out of a little, warning lights need to go off, as we are likely in the presence of spiritual bunkum.

Wait a minute, Crosby. Are you telling me there is no difference between believers and leaders? Are we all peas in a pot of egalitarian soup? Well, yes and no. The issue is one of rank and how rank is defined.

Paul seems to hint at rank among the apostles in Galatians 2:2–9. He uses the terms (King James Version), *reputation, pillars*, referring to the status, rank, or influencing authority among the apostles. It is extremely significant for our discussion that although he *acknowledges* the presence of status, he is *dismissive of it* in terms of significance (Galatians 2:6). Therefore, he acknowledges an evident reality but does not endorse a spiritual order. We cannot press this passage too far.

It is unfortunate that in our culture rank is defined positionally from office and calling and it implies hierarchy and subordination. Since it is not technically a biblical term, I would like to use two alternate words as synonymous with the kingdom quality of rank: the *measure of stature*, or in one word, *maturity.*[7]

We are not all equal in the measure of the stature of Christ—in our inner development. It is possible, and common, to be invested with a church position and possess very little measure of His stature. It is also conversely true that someone can be completely unvested in office, position, title, and function and possess a high order of spiritual rank. A spiritually fresh babe in Christ has more rank than an apostle over a three-hundred-church network who has been too busy to maintain his devotional life for the last three years.

It is appropriate to acknowledge those in Christ, who by reason of "redeemed time" in the faith, have yielded to the processes of God and who incarnate "more of Christ" than you or I might in general or in a specific area. We do not need to categorically subordinate ourselves to them but assume a posture of deference and a readiness to listen. However, merely punching our spiritual-time clock to accrue kingdom seniority does not constitute spiritual rank. What we have *done* with our time in relationship to Christ and our freshness of intimacy with Him[8] determines rank. Rank *is not determined* by position, office, or calling.

We are also not equal in grace endowment. This is clear from the parables of the pounds/talents (King James Version).[9] The master did not distribute equally to each individual. The Holy Spirit distributes His gifts and abilities as He sees fit.[10] Every vessel (believer) is equal in glory and honor but not in grace endowment. Differences in endowment do not, however, determine hierarchical rank. Endowment varies proportionately to assignment—the differences relate to the demands of the assignment! If someone has greater endowment than another, it is not so the greater can maintain positional authority and hierarchy but so the greater can more abundantly supply the other! (Remember, headship is about life supply, not positional hierarchy [see chapter 4]). In the kingdom, demand determines supply! Variation in spiritual endowment is intended for distribution to need in divine assignment, not accrual to positional rank. (Refer to the diagrams at the end of chapter 9.)

We are also not equal in the sphere (scope) of our divine assignment and the responsibilities of that assignment. Romans 12:3 states that everyone is given a measure (Gr. *metron*) of faith. The passage then proceeds to describe how each *metron* is different. It is clear from the Lord's parables of the talents/pounds (King James Version) that there are variations in endowments and variations in the spheres of dominion in proportion to the endowment and how faithful we have been with it. Greater grace (endowment, giftedness) mixed with greater obedience is required for greater spheres of expression. However, this also is not hierarchical; it is functional.

Therefore, defining rank in terms of maturity, endowment, and sphere is legitimate. Defining it from ministry, title, education, talent, skill, office, calling, or position is not. When we acknowledge the maturity, endowment, and sphere of another, including, but not limited to apostles, we are actually acknowledging and yielding to Christ (recognizing Christ within as we spoke of in chapter 2). We can then voluntarily affiliate or align with that manifestation of Christ. An apostle is not entitled to any submission merely because of his apostleship. His authority is limited to the measure of the stature of Christ he possesses, his grace gift endowment, and the limitation of his *metron*. If an apostle is thinking or behaving carnally, operating outside his grace gift, and outside his *metron*, we owe brotherly love—*nothing else.*

Casting the Cast Vision

What about vision casting? Isn't that a basic, fundamental premise of leadership? Well, again, the Scriptures never use the phrase and never associate it with leadership. The case is made at best from Old Testament leadership models (which we have already addressed as inadequate) and an inference from Proverbs 29:18 and Habakkuk 2:2. Proverbs 29:18

says the people perish from a lack of vision. The alleged implication is that good leaders provide vision, or envision their people. In Habakkuk 2:2, it is alleged that good leaders are to "make the vision plain," implying that the set-man's vision must be clearly and strongly presented so every one can align with it. In application it is like this: "God's order is the envisioning of his leaders and the submission of the people to their envisioned leader. As your leader, God has given me the vision and direction for your lives in God, as the people of God. Now, *if you are really* a son of my heart and a son of this house and submit to the house vision, you will, or we expect you to, or we hope you will, ———," or variations on this theme.

Proverbs 29:18

There are two problems with the classic interpretation and application of this verse:

1. Importing western value systems into the text.
2. Preaching it out of context. The second half of the verse is rarely mentioned in leadership forums.

Projecting western cultural and leadership values onto the biblical text gives it a meaning that has no basis in exegetical reality. The verse has *nothing to do with* esoteric visions, inspirations, projects, goals, and "the mission statement" of an executive leader. The passage refers to spiritual and prophetic insight into the Word of God, specifically the Torah, as the second half of the verse contextually makes clear. *God's people perish not from failure to submit to the set man's dreams of kingdom accomplishments but rather from failure to have spiritual and prophetic insight into the Word of God!* The lack of restraint refers to living apart from the constraints of God's moral law as revealed by prophetic insight through the prophets,[11] not by refusing to give one's self to the vision of the house! The former is legitimate and makes total sense; the latter is a modern imagination.

Christ and Him crucified and equipping the saints *is the vision* of the New Covenant era! A "visionary" leader is not one who necessarily sees and accomplishes great things to be admired by man. That which is highly esteemed by man is an abomination to God. Shoot, you don't need the Holy Spirit to accomplish great things. You can do it with a winsome and warm personality, the skills of a used car salesman, the passion of a teary-eyed evangelist, pictures of a few starving children, and graduation certificates from Dale Carnegie and Tony Robbins.

Habakkuk 2:2

Make the vision plain upon tables that he may run that readeth it.

Isn't part of being a leader being visionary, making the vision plain? Well, again, this is not a leadership verse. The context (*isn't context a theological party pooper!*) has to do with the Lord answering Habakkuk's specific prayer concerning the nature of injustice. The "vision" the prophet receives is of the Messianic Age when God will finally defeat His enemies and restore righteousness and justice in the earth.

Now, if being a "visionary leader" means making Messiah (Christ), His ultimate victory, and His kingdom rule plain before all, then I agree! I want to be a visionary leader! However, most who consider themselves visionary or revelatory don't read the verse as "make the vision *plain*," they read it as "*make* the vision." The vision has already been made for us. It is Christ and Him crucified. The leader's job is to make Him plain, not put forward his or her grand dreams with which subordinates must comply. If being visionary means having lots of grand and great ideas, plans and dreams to accomplish "for God" if the necessary troops will just submit to it (and keep the tithe and offering flowing—maybe we can send a "free love-gift"), you will have to look elsewhere for a justifying Scripture. This one doesn't do it. The annoying detail of so many "visionary" dreams is that they usually have the delightful side effect of making our kingdom great as well as the Lord's—maybe even greater.

Don Rumble captures the spiritual essence of correct local church vision:

> The local church is not to express simply the mind of its leadership, its prophets, its administrators, etc. The local church is where Christ arises in the midst of His People. As we "tap into" the flow of His life, *His mind* is revealed. The Church is to constantly experience *more than* the expectation of its leadership, *more than* the visions of its prophets and *more than* the strategies of its apostles. The purpose of God for each gathering is greater than our abilities to quantify and define.[12]

Having great "revelations" or being "revelatory" does not in itself make someone apostolic. Apostolic revelation does not function in a vacuum. To be biblical, it must have an object: Christ and Him crucified. Being apostolic and visionary is about seeing Him clearly, and from that sight, facilitating sight in others.[13] Even the eighth-century Irish monk, Dallan Forgaill, understood this when he wrote (verses one and four):

> Be Thou my Vision, O Lord of my heart;
> Naught be all else to me, save that Thou art
> Thou my best Thought, by day or by night,
> Waking or sleeping, Thy presence my light.
> Riches I heed not, nor man's empty praise,
> Thou mine Inheritance, now and always:
> Thou and Thou only, first in my heart,
> High King of Heaven, my Treasure Thou art.

Christ and Him crucified *is the vision*. Oh, I forgot, Brother Forgaill was not part of the emerging, cutting-edge, new-reformation, revolutionary, wealth-transferring, revelation-birthing, foundation-shaking, radical warrior, and last-day company of world-changing prophets and apostles. He probably had a poverty spirit that darkened his mind to understanding. He must have needed a covering apostle to bring him into the full blessing of insight. Oh, all right, I'll stop. But really, listen to us talk. Isn't our language just *plain silly* and our opinions of ourselves a *tad inflated*?

How much "government" does it take to facilitate "love God and others as yourself"? The goal of a godly leader is not to set the vision so others can follow it but to equip the saints to fulfill their vision. The house of God is, by definition, full of multiple visions, because the Spirit envisions each member with personal destiny. Think about this from a purely pragmatic and "fruit-bearing" point of view. If you were God and wanted to get the most done in the quickest time, would you have two thousand people facilitating one man's vision and goal or one man facilitating two thousand visions and goals? Which would accomplish more? The former builds *our* kingdom; the latter builds *His*. God's kingdom increases through death and resurrection and the scattering of seed. Man's kingdom is built by gathering people in unity of vision and purpose to accomplish a great goal. God takes a pretty dim view of that thinking. He calls it Babylon.[14]

The practical problem arises from our corporate and business structures rather than anything inherently spiritual. Leader ego issues play in to the allocation of corporate resources (money, people, and time). Multiple "visions" cannot be accommodated ("If I fund theirs, I can't fund mine"). So much vision-casting rhetoric is about where money is spent and who controls that decision. That is more a reality of our manmade corporate structures than an inherent biblical principle of leadership. It is not inherently evil. It is just a reality of a self-inflicted problem due to our structures, not divine mandate. The reality cannot be used as justification for ungodly authority structures.

Now there is nothing wrong with mutually cooperating with, or voluntarily aligning one's self, with a leader to help him or her accomplish a large divine task: smallness is not necessarily holy, and largeness is not necessarily success (*except in the new apostolic reformation!*). However, it is *not legitimate* to *require* people to do so in submission to a misguided and dubious principle of coming under authority, covering, and biblical headship! It is also illegitimate to spiritually, psychologically, or socially marginalize folks who will not "sign the covenant pledge to support leadership vision," or who do not want to be "a spiritual son or daughter," or do not share the passion for the "house vision."

How can you tell if you are in an abusive leadership situation, disguised as submission to authority, covering, and the set man's vision? Practice a powerful tool God has given you: *say no.* That's it—not in a bad spirit or defiance and not concerning apostolic doctrine over sin, but in all other areas, politely and firmly say no when it is authentic to say *no.* Be real. Be who you are. Be what God has made you to be. Tell a leader *no* sometime and watch how he or she responds to you. If you feel the icy flow of withdrawal, separation, and suspicion come upon you, get out of Dodge before the sun hits the horizon. If on the other hand you are respected, dignified, and perhaps engaged with in further dialogue, you may have found a healthy local church home.

One of the most liberating things I ever did as a local church pastor was give people under my care the explicit, articulated, right to tell me *no*, and the right to disagree with me. It was remarkable to watch the effect it had. It was not "jailbreak of the carnal unsubmitted" as many of my more authoritarian friends dread as an inevitability. Rather, gospel liberty and genuine identity in Christ emerged from years of suppression under authoritarian, rigid, and legal styles of leadership. Peace, harmony, unity, oneness, and yes, order resulted. Some with literally decades of experience in the church were shocked that it was actually "all right" to tell me *no.* Of course it is all right! I am their pastor, not their God! The reason the result was so positive is because I was not there trying to implement "the vision God gave me" but rather to release people into the vision God gave *them.* People intuitively know when you are genuinely "for them." It is amazing how conflict subsides and order sets in when liberty and personal dignity instead of government and authority are preached and practiced. The former is the kingdom norm; the latter is for crisis.

My wife and I had a couple in our home once for some relationship building and personal life plan discussion. They were a very seasoned and mature couple having spent almost their entire lives from their earliest youth in the apostolic/charismatic brand of the church. They had served faithfully in multiple capacities over the years. In the course of the conversation, as my wife and I started inquiring how we could help bring them into the realization of their dreams, the wife broke down and started crying. She said that it was the first time in over forty years of church life that they had experienced a pastor/leader expressing actual concern for them as individuals, rather than asking them what they could do for "the ministry." I suggest that her experience is not isolated, but tragically closer to the norm in hard-charging, discipleship oriented, "doing something for God" type of churches.

Apostolic Strategies

> Who then is Paul, and who is Apollos, but ministers by whom ye believed, even as the Lord gave to every man? I have planted, Apollos watered; but God gave the increase. So then neither is he that plants any thing, neither he that waters; but God that gives the increase. Now he that plants and he that waters are one: and every man shall receive his own reward according to his own labor. For we are laborers together with God: ye are God's husbandry, ye are God's building. According to the grace of God which is given unto me, as a wise masterbuilder, I have laid the foundation, and another builds thereon. But let every man take heed how he builds thereupon. For other foundation can no man lay than that is laid, which is Jesus Christ.
>
> (1 Corinthians 3:5–11)

In this passage, Paul writes to *correct* the Corinthians for what the apostolic movement considers *normative*: alignment with a single apostle. I think it worth the ink to reemphasize the plain, straightforward, context of the passage that we already hinted at in chapter 4. Different factions were jockeying in the church for what would be called today "apostolic alignment": "I am of Apollos, I am of Paul." In modern terms, it would be:

- Paul is my covering apostle, and he should be yours, too.
- Apollos is my spiritual father, and he should be yours, too
- Peter is my primary source of apostolic download, and he should be yours, too. You can only have one apostolic source.

Paul rebukes and corrects the Corinthians for this kind of thinking! The apostolic movement wants to *revive it* as the "new apostolic governmental order!" We need to examine this passage.

The term *master builder* can legitimately define one of the qualities of an apostle. The question is builder of what? By implication, apostles are said to be uniquely called and gifted to strategically build the church and various kingdom structures throughout the earth. It is undoubtedly true that strategic design and tactical abilities can make up an apostolic ministry.[15] However, applying the language (master builder) from this passage to apostles while *ignoring* the *context* and implications of the passage's *ethics* is a problem.

The Insignificance of the Apostle (1 Corinthians 3:5-7)

Paul is crystal clear that the apostolic builder is *nothing* (verses 5-7). The one who plants and the one who waters are of *no significance*. God is the ultimate builder, the One who assures a crop (mixing metaphors, as does the passage). The current apostolic movement is starkly—*180 degrees*—out of phase with this ethic. As currently structured, the set-man apostle (and submission to him) is *the necessity* of a network! Rallying around an envisioning apostle is what defines a network! The network's reason for existence is to implement the set apostle's vision, without which there would be no network! Far from insignificant, the apostle, and proper alignment to the apostle, is the *sine qua non*[16] of alleged kingdom operations.

1. **Unity** (1 Corinthians 3:8). In current apostolic network structures, unity is logically and spiritually impossible. In spite of all our claims to humility, equality, and kingdom purpose, many apostles remain extremely possessive and territorial under the guise of the need for singularity of vision and purpose. Because most networks are institutionally based on facilitating the "set-man's vision" (which is largely task-, target-, and mission-oriented) *by definition*, they cannot accommodate any intrusion of "*visionary otherness*," because otherness will dilute the set man's vision. If the singularity of our vision is Christ and Him crucified and the empowerment and facilitation of others, unity becomes a very simple and achievable reality.

   Also, because the churches and pastors in a given network are usually the apostle's financial support stream, there is *no chance* an apostle is going to let someone else in and take pieces of his pie! I have heard the term *cash cows* used to describe the financial support churches bring to apostolic networks. It is offensive and indicative of how corrupt the movement is. Role inversion occurs. Rather than the apostles serving the churches, the churches exist to support the apostles.

   I am not talking about inviting a guest minister in to do a weekend seminar. I am talking about allowing another to functionally and spiritually build into the fabric of the lives of a local church—to have a place in the hearts and pocketbooks of the people—allowing someone else to shape the spiritual DNA in a local assembly. This is inherently threatening and contrary to the deficient and limited "spiritual fathering" metaphors that are used to describe pastoral and kingdom ministry (i.e. you can only have "one father").

   If we desire to impart Christ's DNA into people, we could care less who does it. If we want "our DNA" (a phrase I hear used repeatedly) in the people, in contrast to "someone else's DNA," we will never touch true spiritual unity. Both Jesus and Paul could care less about who, what, and how the gospel was preached.[17] Our territorialness results from the possessive ownership and pride-filled self-estimation of how valuable our particular spiritual niche is—our "spiritual inheritance," "our distinctive." So rather than preaching Christ and Him crucified, we preach our distinctive. We try to get people to rally around it as we build our networks and blindly facilitate a cult—a religious group that no longer has Christ and Him crucified as their center. This ethos is *corrupt*. This ethos is *anti-christ*.

A friend of mine used to say, "We would be amazed at what could be accomplished for Christ if no one cared who got the credit." Current apostolic network structures simply cannot accommodate true Pauline unity.

2. **Validation** (1 Corinthians 3:8). It is God who determines value and reward. A true apostle does not need the presence of an organization for personal validation needs. The changed lives of people and their immovable planting on the Sure Foundation are enough. The changed lives of people are the seal of apostleship, not the size of my network and how many churches I may have "under me."

3. **Issues of ownership and control** (v.9). It is explicitly clear from this verse that Paul did not take personal ownership of what he was building. The people and the church in Corinth were not "*his*." They were not part of *his* network but rather a part of God's kingdom. Paul did not insist on "covering and control" over them. He did not require territorial rights to the churches in which he laid the foundation. This quality is starkly missing in the emergent apostolic movement. It is "assumed" that churches must remain "aligned" to the apostle (code for "in relationship to me, and me only, as the primary covering apostle") for the existence of the life of the church. Paul laid a foundation and let someone else build upon it. He did not hinder another apostle's influence on the people.

The vision of many so-called apostolic strategists is the accumulation and agglomeration of authority, wealth, and resources into their circle of influence, to the exclusion of others; all under the assumption that the activity is "for Jesus." There is nothing inherently corrupt in building well with intelligence, wisdom, strategy, and tactics. There is nothing inherently wrong with projects and dreams that are vast and large in scope. There is nothing wrong with the necessary organization and finances to see these goals accomplished. However, the line between divinely-mandated goals and the mere expansion of the human soul looking for validation and significance is frequently crossed.

How does the Lord energize great dreams and at the same time prevent their corruption? By applying Calvary to the issue of ownership. When personal "ownership" seeps under the door of our soul like fog in a scene from a cheap mystery movie, we are corrupted. When our hands cling too tightly to what the Lord has built through us, when the network is *mine* and under *my* covering and under *my* direction and under *my* vision and under *my* headship and in submission to *my* leadership, it is *corrupt;* even though it may seemingly produce great kingdom results. These labors are the wood, hay, and stubble that Paul guarantees will be burned up, and the laborers those Jesus does not recognize.[18]

4. **The correct foundation** (v. 11). Someone who is a master builder according to the biblical pattern in Paul's life is not someone who builds a network around personal charisma, giftedness, and task-specific mandate. An apostolic master builder is someone supernaturally graced to see the foundation of Jesus Christ built into every believer and every local church. All tasks must serve the goal of the revelation of Christ within people, not become the goal. Apostolic building is a spiritual quality that results in the increase of Christ and His kingdom in the earth, not necessarily the increase of the network. The two do not always coincide. Paul's apostolic mandate was to make Christ known in a foundational way. The call of an apostle is to be gladly spent and used up by others, not build a great network (2 Corinthians 12:12–15).

The building systems of the emergent apostolic movement are theologically unsound, methodologically flawed, and ethically tainted. Rather than celebrating their emergence in a spirit of restoration and reformation, we should be bemoaning that so many are being duped by another gospel, another kingdom, and another king.

CHAPTER 8

CHURCH GOVERNMENT: AS CLEAR AS MUD

A Leader Is . . . Not . . .

A leader is not the chief visionary. A leader is not the chief executive. A leader is someone who accepts the stress and strain of the present inconvenience of service in order to bring the ones he/she serves to fullness of destiny. A leader works hard, sacrifices, is regularly criticized and rarely rewarded; yet does not fall into functional atheism, which is the belief that ultimate responsibility for everything rests with him/her. He or she is someone who can bring Christ's resurrection life out of a situation when others cannot. A Christian leader is someone who is unalterably Christ-centered and who has ability to bring others into alignment with the person of Christ and the purposes of Christ in their life. A leader is someone psychologically, volitionally, and physically aligned and identified with Christ's kingdom interests in others, not the leader's interests in other people. A leader is not necessarily

- the one with the most information,
- the most gifted,
- the most talented,
- the most educated,

- the most correct in a situation,
- the one with position.

Leadership is a calling.[1] If you are not called, you dare not lead, and if you are called, you dare *not* lead![2] Do not let insecurity and desire for personal validation drive you to pursue leadership. If the only way you can feel good about yourself is when you lead, you probably ought not to lead. Your value and identity in Christ is the basis of mental well being, not what you can accomplish for Him through your gifts and talents. You must know who you are apart from what you can do, accomplish, or perform. If you have no sense of personhood apart from task, you do not belong in Christian leadership. You belong under therapeutic care. There is no surer way into the spiritual ditch than to engage in Christian leadership with unresolved psychological issues of personal identity.

There is nothing wrong with passion and drive. It is the inner power of propulsion God put in humanity for achievement. However, in its uncrucified form, it is just so much human energy. God does not want to extinguish your passion. He wants to arrest it, sentence it, kill it, and resurrect it on the lines of Calvary, and the Holy Spirit is the marshal of the kingdom; armed with Calvary's arrest warrant, He always gets His man and faithfully executes the death sentence on Adam. Fortunately, the hand that pulls the lever on the electric chair is the hand that raises up again.

The foundation of Christian leadership is a Calvary paradigm, not visionary principles and management skills. Christian leadership is the call to experience His death and His resurrection power, at depths and levels of which you have not dreamed, on behalf of others. We should look to the Word and Spirit, not the business and management world, for leadership metaphors. The direction of influence should be from faith to business, not business to faith. A Christian leader has upon him or her the aroma of Christ.[3] When others are around you, they are fed by the Christ in you. In a sense, they taste you and see that the Lord is good.[4] If your being hated, misunderstood, slandered, lied about, let down, lonely, rejected, abused, betrayed, and abandoned doesn't bother you, and you wake up every morning with a burning desire to serve God and His people in any way, you might be called to lead. If the burning love of Christ constrains you to voluntarily say, "Lord, I take it and take it gladly for your cause in your people," you might be called. If you would rather do something else, you should.

Christian leadership operates in a climate of mutuality: leaders empower, followers cooperate (submit). Leadership authority properly exercised is the ability to serve and empower others, not the right to rule them. It is knowing, developing, and releasing others into divine destiny. It is inherently relational. You cannot empower others if you do not know their gifts, calling, talents, skills, and limitations. That is why you cannot effectively "father" from a distance. You cannot invest yourself into someone you see once a year. That is a visit, not an investment. You can care for them, you can help them, you can minister to them, but you cannot father them. You can oversee an organization from a distance, but you cannot father. Oswald Chambers says the true love of God is very practical. All the rest is just sentimental talk.[5]

Clear, Translucent, and Opaque

As we said very early in this text, when it comes to structure and form of church government, the Scriptures can be annoyingly vague. It is difficult using the book of Acts as a "standard" for church government because it was a transitional and emergent time. Folks from both traditions (episcopal and congregational governments) appeal to the book of Acts as the authority for their convictions. I doubt very much if folks who try to find an eternal pattern in the book of Acts believe that meeting in synagogues or shaving our heads and taking oaths are something we need to do today because "that is what they did in Acts." Many things in Acts were just the historical and cultural realities of the time they were in and have no application beyond that. It can be difficult to definitively separate those practices and beliefs that were limited and local from those eternal and universal. How much was adapted to circumstance and how much was meant as an eternal pattern is a tough call at times.

In Paul's epistles, there are some character qualifications for elders. There are also descriptions of their tasks and function throughout the Word (e.g. Titus 1:5ff; 1 Timothy 5:17ff; 1 Peter 5:1ff; Acts 20:28ff; James 5:13–15). However, the Scriptures are less specific on how they related among themselves and with the Ephesians 4 ministries. There are glimpses and hints but not a lot of detail. There is barely any hard and fast governmental form to which we can point our finger and say, "There, that is how you do it! That's definitively how it is done!"

It is also interesting that in the Gospels our Lord is silent on the matter of church structure and government. He speaks of the *values* that constitute His government in many passages. The ethics of His kingdom saturate the Gospels, but there is next to nothing on structural specifics. Rigidity is always a mistake when arguing from silence. But knowing who He was, one has to wonder if there was not purpose in His silence. I wonder if His concern is with *how* we do things rather than *what* we do? That is, form and method do not come near spirit and attitude in importance. Knowing that His gospel applies to all peoples in all places and cultures for all time, could these things have been left intentionally vague? I think this is at least a possibility and perhaps should soften our dogmatism and opinions on those governmental structures that are supposedly "blessed" (or contingent for blessing) and those that are allegedly not so.

What do we explicitly know from Scripture? Paul ordained elders/presbyters/bishops to oversee the affairs of the local churches he founded. They were also uniquely Paul's representatives, Paul's "ambassadors," to the local assembly during Paul's absence. Concerning local church government, the Scriptures are *clear on ethics, translucent on function, and nearly opaque on form.* What made the Pauline churches work was not their governmental structure *but their relationship to Paul.* Where there was no relationship, there was no government, even though a person might maintain his/her grace endowment and calling. There seems to be a lack of "order and command structure." Some people seem to stay "aligned" with Paul and others did not.

At the end of his life, the only worker physically left with Paul is Luke. I find it difficult to believe that every other worker who came "out from Paul's apostolic mantle and covering" was ineffective (not blessed) for the rest of their lives because they violated the principle of spiritual covering! It may have been, and likely was, personally painful for Paul, but he makes no comment about his authority as their "covering" apostle and their "responsibility" to "stay aligned governmentally" with him. He simply releases the whole matter to God.

> For Demas hath forsaken me, having loved this present world, and is departed unto Thessalonica; Crescens to Galatia, Titus unto Dalmatia. Only Luke is with me. Take Mark, and bring him with thee: for he is profitable to me for the ministry. And Tychicus have I sent to Ephesus . . . At my first answer no man stood with me, but all men forsook me: I pray God that it may not be laid to their charge.
>
> (2 Timothy 4:10–16)

Elevated Elders

> This is a true saying, If a man desire the office of a bishop, he desireth a good work.
>
> (1 Timothy 3:1)

Some think the terms *bishop, presbyter,* and *elder* are identical and some do not. It seems that in the early days there may have been a distinction between elders and bishops. It is also difficult to make a clear-cut delineation between the Ephesian 4 ministries and the bishops or presbyters. In at least one case, Peter's, we know he served in both capacities.[6]

I think that sometimes the problem we have navigating these things relates to the elevation of the role of an elder that the Scriptures do not sustain. Let's look at what the Scriptures are explicit about: character qualifications. Because this is fairly familiar territory, I will combine the character qualification lists in Timothy and Titus and a thought or two from 1 Peter with some expanded definitions.[7] I have a reason for outlining them like this here.

1. "Blameless, not accused of riot, just, innocent." This does not mean faultless or perfect but someone against whom no charge of immorality or of holding false doctrine is alleged or someone facing a legal indictment charge for carousing, etc. In this sense, someone above reproach. "Blameless" is a metaphor taken from the case of an expert and skillful boxer who so defends every part of his body so that it is impossible for his antagonist to give one hit—nothing sticks, no charge can be laid at his feet.

2. "Husband of one wife." There are many opinions on this phrase. Literally it means a "one-woman man." Likely it is not limited to one's marriage status but has the broader meaning of not having a wandering eye.

3. "Vigilant." This means "sober," especially as it relates to drink and wine; circumspect, especially as it relates to drink; temperate in behavior.

4. "Sober, self-controlled." This can be confusing for us, as it is not related to alcohol. It means "sound in mind and self controlled; prudent; having passions under control."

5. "Good behavior, self controlled." This means "orderly, decorous, modest, and mannerly, self-restrained, not given to unbridled passions."

6. "Given to hospitality, lover of good, virtuous." Fond of guests; literally, lover of strangers, lover of good and virtuous humanity.

7. "Apt to teach, able to exhort and correct, convince." This means "able to impart instruction and bring correction." The form and nature of the instruction is not specified.

8. "Not given to wine." Not a tippler, not frequenting the wine bottle.

9. "Not a striker, not given to anger." Not quarrelsome, easy to get along with, not contentious. Someone who is frequently in

conflict is not ready yet to be a leader, perhaps not called to be one.

10. "Filthy lucre." This particular attribute listing is textually very weak in the Greek manuscripts, and it is covered under covetousness below. Greedy, sordid, loving money, pursuing money as a goal, using any and all means to enrich ones self.

11. "Patient, not self-willed." Mild, forbearing, opposite of quarrelsome.

12. "Not a brawler." Not quarrelsome, prone to fighting, contentious, apt to make peace, choosing reconciliation over conflict.

13. "Covetousness." The love of money is the root of all evil. It is akin to idolatry, the love of money and things.

14. "Ruling his own house well, children in subjection." The word for *rule* is the Greek *proistemi*, which, as we have seen earlier, is not quite as authoritative as it first sounds: "go before, stand before."

15. "Holy." This does not mean consecrated in a religious sense, nor right in relationship to human laws. It means "inherently right." In a Christian context, it would be in right relationship to God and man. At least someone who has been "made right" at the new birth.

16. "Gravity." Honor, respect; having a household characterized by mutual respect. The gravity applies to the elder, not the children. It means "being serious, having a 'handle on life.'" It is not about certain personality traits or a false piety.

17. "Not a novice." Not a new convert. This does not imply some sort of age limitation or some mandatory tenure.

18. "A good report of them that are without." We are to consider the opinions of unbelievers when appointing elders—bosses, co-workers, unsaved relatives. I know of only a few churches that take this seriously.

19. "Holding fast the Word." Trustworthy in doctrine, doctrinally sound to core gospel precepts.

20. "Steward of God." Trustworthy; responsible for running the affairs of the "house;" one who oversees "household distributions."

I want to add just a few expanding comments.

Calling and Desire

Godly character alone does not solely qualify someone as an elder. The calling and placement of the Holy Spirit precedes character qualifications.[8] Character is developable; calling is not. Calling is discoverable, but not developable. Because I have been loyal and faithful does not make me elder material. Too many people are ordained to eldership because of loyalty, faithfulness, and service, only to experience grief and pain because of lack of calling. God's grace follows God's calling. If we overlook this point, we are in for big trouble and personal pain. In the heat of battle, the elder who is present because of faithfulness rather than calling will not stand, because there is no supernatural grace available.

It is also not sinful to desire eldership.[9] Calling manifests itself in desire. God births, crucifies, resurrects, delays, and fulfills desire all at the same! Many insecure leaders mistakenly view any shred of initiative or ambition in a subordinate as a manifestation of the Adamic nature. They genuinely view it their divine mandate to crush initiative in individuals to teach them "humility" and the "disciplines of the cross."

This is a gross corruption of the message of the crucified-life that actually energizes a performance-based spirit and a criminal mentality that thinks if I faithfully and humbly comply with today's present limitations and restrictions, the day will eventually come when the limitations will be removed and I will be "released into ministry" by the presiding warden, er, I mean overseeing minister. *Solely* denying desire in an individual will *never produce* the inner transformation to Christ-likeness and holiness the Scriptures speak of.

Docility is not a virtue. Passivity is not Christlike. I have heard it said that anyone who expresses interest in leadership (office of an elder/

bishop) automatically proves he is not qualified because he has asked for the office! His initiation supposedly disqualifies him! His ambition is esteemed carnal. Disinterest is viewed as if it were the tenth fruit of the Spirit. The *Scripture says* that someone who desires (stretches out, reaches for, grasps, extends, gives everything, wrestles, agonizes) the office of leadership (elder, bishop) *desires* a good thing![10] Church culture says be polite, don't put yourself forward, let the Holy Spirit decide those things, etc.

Apt to Teach

Being apt to teach does not mean an elder must be a theologian or an exegete. You can teach in more ways than lecture and classroom. That is a Western, Gentile understanding, not an Eastern, biblical understanding of teaching. Eastern teaching is impartational through relationship, not intellectually through the classroom. Just because someone has superior Bible knowledge does not automatically make that person qualified to lead or teach. We teach out from our lives, not our knowledge.

Apt to teach means the simple ability to disciple others in the basics of the faith through example, word, and deed. It does not mean the capacity to thrill and amaze with Bible revelation! It does not mean an elder must have a pulpit gift expression. Too often someone who develops abilities in the Word, who serves faithfully and loyally, becomes an elder without even discussing the matter of calling, gift mix, or temperament. Apt to teach is a quality of spirit and character, not the acquisition of biblical knowledge sanctified by tenure in the church and offerings in the plate. Someone could be a wonderful Bible teacher and have neither grace, nor gift, nor temperament to be an elder.

The correction element of apt to teach (Titus: exhort and convince) is one of the biggest absences in elders that I know. Our politically-correct, non-judgmental, secular culture is a non-confrontational culture. Unfortunately, so is the dominant American church culture. The ability to bring reproof and correction is as fundamental to being an elder as loving and caring. Too many elders do not have the heart for the psychological heavy lifting of confronting sinful behavior. Their overly pastoral and passive attitude is: "Let's just love and pray for them, and perhaps the Lord will take care of the problem." This is deception. Anyone who cannot confront, when necessary, is not elder material, regardless of how much he may know about the ten toes of the beast and regardless of how big a "loving heart" he[11] may have. We do not have to enjoy confrontation, and we do not have to make it our specialty, but we do have to be able to do it in a spirit of grace and truth if we want to be an elder.

Having the Home in Order

This does not mean having "perfect" children, or a "perfect" marriage.[12] If either were the case, no one would be an elder. I know of a situation where a man had eleven children. He and his wife raised, without major problems, ten who served the Lord in their adolescence and adulthood. But one went "sideways" and did not. The leadership at the time told the man he had to step down as an elder because his "family was not in order, under his rule with all gravity." It was, as you might expect, devastating to the man. Too often people whose adolescent children are in rebellion find this verse used against them. The text has nothing to do with that.

Adolescence didn't exist in the first century. It is a modern twentieth-century phenomenon. For a Jewish male you went from childhood to adulthood at your bar mitzvah. You were not an adolescent at thirteen; you were an adult. This is due in part to the fact that life span was short! Seventy-five percent of the population was dead by the age of twenty-six, and ninety percent were dead by the age of forty-six![13] You did not have time for adolescent angst over whether or not Bobby, the captain of the football team, is going to ask you to the prom! You were too busy trying to get food to eat or survive disease! The fact that in our culture individuals of the ages thirteen to eighteen are minors should not be carried over into interpretations of this verse. If you want to be strictly "biblical," having an adolescent in the home is having another adult in the home, not a child. The verse does not apply.

How are we to interpret and apply these eldership qualities? Paul made three complete missionary journeys in eleven years. He planted multiple churches throughout Asia Minor, modern-day Greece and Italy. He was in cities eighteen to thirty-six months and from heathen, pagan, stone-worshiping idolaters he had his subordinates ordain elders. Eighteen to thirty-six months! What is the implication of this fact?

We need to be careful not to elevate the role of elders, in either expectation or requirement, above what the Scriptures actually teach. We need to seriously reevaluate what an elder is and does. In many of our churches, apostolic and otherwise, considering someone who is not first a "son" as elder material is unheard of. It would take years, if not decades for the individual to prove unwavering loyalty to the set man. How does this practice square with the fact that Paul appointed elders after a few months of ministry, not a few years? There is something categorically "unbiblical" in our methodologies concerning appointment of elders. What are some of the "extra-biblical' requirements we put on people in order to be elders?

- They must be sons of the house.
- They must be sons of the vision.
- They must faithfully serve my vision first.
- They must agree with the house vision.
- They must not ———— (fill in the blank with sin or conviction of choice!).
- They must be tithers.
- They must be able to make executive decisions.

The list could go on and on. We add endless extra-biblical requirements for elders because we define the term *governmentally* rather than by function. We think of it in terms of a position and office rather than as a ministerial function. We are uncomfortable giving people "governmental authority" that is executive, decision-making authority. So we add to the clear biblical requirements a list of standards that cannot be met unless the individual sells his soul and sacrifices his identity on the altar of the set man's dreams.

What do the Scriptures really say? Well, if we categorized and summed up the qualities listed in Scripture, it seems pretty basic, not insignificant, but basic:

- Don't be a drunk. (The 1 Timothy list puts a lot of emphasis on that; it was a major cultural concern at the time, as they lived on eighteen hundred calories a day with 25% of their calories coming from alcohol. Drunkenness would be a major problem.[14])
- Don't be a fornicator (blameless, sexual and marital fidelity).
- Not someone facing trial (*blameless* had legal connotations; someone against whom there was no legal charge).
- Don't be a crook (money, filthy lucre, covetousness).
- Don't be violent (striker, brawler).
- Behave decently, be friendly (gravity, patient, hospitality, good).
- Be converted but not a new convert (not a novice).
- Be able to help someone else to walk in Christ (apt to teach).
- Get along on the job (testimony from without).

Folks, this is not rocket science. This is not setting the bar so high that only the glow-in-the-dark saints qualify. Think about this: How "mature" or "spiritual" could the elders in Ephesus and Corinth be after only eighteen to thirty-six months of "leadership training?" Our concept and Paul's concept of what a novice is are apparently not too close! Let's phrase it this way. How spiritual were you a year and a half after your salvation? Ready to be an elder? Well, either our standards are too high (likely) or the first-century church had something on the ball more than we do (also likely). The point is that you do not have to be a water-walking wonder to be an elder. We have inflated eldership to a level the Scriptures never intended it to be.

CHAPTER 9

CONCLUSIONS

Salman Rushdie describes the essence of fundamentalism (all brands) as having nothing to do with religion and everything to do with power[1]—not a bad insight. The use and abuse of power could subtitle human history, in and out of the church. The primal temptation at its core was an appeal to power/authority: Godlikeness.[2] How power is handled differentiates Christ's kingdom from a cult. You do not have to play with snakes, cut off chicken's heads, or have wild sex orgies to be in a cult. Effective cults are more subtle than that. Two foundational characteristics of a cult are 1) disempowerment of the individual, and 2) the discouragement of self-initiative and self-thought under the guise of submission to authority. Cults disempower individuals and empower a limited class of specialists; or in the worst manifestation, a specialist— singular,[3] to whom the masses must submit. The specialists supposedly possess unique abilities unavailable to the masses. Therefore, the masses must rely on the specialist(s) for access to insight, spiritual realities, or other alleged blessings as part of the cultic ritual and order.

In every cult there is a governing authority (someone who establishes and enforces order) and a mystic authority (someone who has access into divine mysteries). Inherent with these powers is the ability to reward and punish. By compliance (submission), individuals are rewarded by the governing authorities (access to leadership, access to ministry opportunities, access to the "father's heart," etc.). By acting in ways that mimic the behavior and values of the empowered classes, people can achieve a false sense of identity and community that lets them feel empowered, though not genuinely so. This is why, in the church, it is imperative that our governmental structures must have as their ultimate goal the empowerment of individuals, not their submission to authority figures.

In the emerging apostolic movement, the apostles assume governing authority, and the prophets provide mystic authority. Individuals must come under their covering, into "governmental alignment," in order to access various forms of alleged spiritual blessing—the reward of compliance. It is painfully self-evident that this is cultic. In a Christian context, this false process masquerades as discipleship, accountability, and submission to authority. Conformity is not to Christ but to the leadership image and expectations. It promotes dependency and powerlessness.

Leanne Payne rightly recognizes that one of the characteristics of a cult is toward ego and a drive toward personal power in a man or woman that appeals to the masses of the unaffirmed and to the mind-set of our narcissistic age.[4] One of the telltale signs of cultic behavior is the refusal to elevate believers into an adult position but rather insistence on maintaining a childish posture of dependence[5] on someone else to tell them how to act, think, and believe.[6] By abdicating personal power and their own authority, individual wills atrophy under the sway of authoritarian and specialist ministries who claim for themselves special status as representing God's cutting-edge revelation.[7]

This is not Christ's gospel. In His kingdom, authority figures are servants who empower, not specialists who promote dependency. Christ's kingdom is one of equalization—every valley filled, every mountain brought low—not a kingdom of empowered and disempowered classes. There are many practices and beliefs in the church (prophetic, apostolic, and otherwise) that are passionately held as "gospel" which, at the very least, need to be rethought and re-examined for spiritual legitimacy and method of implementation, and perhaps altogether abandoned.

Legitimate kingdom authority always empowers and is always restrained. It is like a train on tracks. The rails, by nature and design, restrain the train. However, because the rails are "suited" for the train they actually empower it. The train has no hope of realization without the tracks. The tracks are necessary to release all the potential of the train. If a train decides to believe it is an airplane, to get an opinion of itself not suited to reality or designed limitation, and attempts to leave its tracks, disaster results.

In the kingdom, love and empowering service are the restraining tracks of authority. Without them, apostolic authority is a diesel in free fall. To be kingdom legitimate, the emerging apostolic must be defined by the restraint of authority (both *dúnamis* and *exousía*), not its expansion. The necessity of the hour is assuring that the tracks of love and service are secure in the rail bed of Christ and Him crucified, not that the apostolic engine gets more horsepower. However, restraint is not the same as limitation. The tracks do not limit the train; they facilitate the train. If the train wants more horsepower to go faster and carry more—fine—no problem! Strengthen the rails and rail bed first!

The essence of the kingdom is endowment and divestment. We are endowed to give away. God the Father, the ultimate source of life, authority, and power, *gave* a Son.[8] The Son divested Himself of glory for the sake of others.[9] The accumulation of authority and power in individuals (apostles or otherwise) and institutions is, and always will be, corrupting, *unless* the accumulation is structured (mindsets, value systems, and methods) *to be given away*. We also need to assure that those values that we export for public consumption are kingdom approved—not personal preferences and cultural projections.

Power sharing is the mandate of the kingdom. Insecure apostles will feel threatened when called upon to divest themselves of their authority. They will feel like they are losing a piece of personal property: "their people," "their churches," "their network," "their rank," "their authority," etc. *That is how it should feel, because God is trying to dismantle a corrupt inner value system contrary to His kingdom.* That is the way God's kingdom works. We gain what we give away (lose) and lose what we hold on to.[10] Authority is given to be given away. *This is the governmental order of God's kingdom, not submission and alignment to covering apostles.*

It has been my great joy and privilege to know a few genuine apostles, who in the spirit of Christ and Him crucified and Abraham's walk up Moriah, have put to death (not for a "season," not with one hand out of the grave, but put to death!) their entire networks and their relationship to them. The sad part is such quality individuals are the exception, not the rule. Expansion of real authority and Christ's kingdom is always the inevitable result. It is just not always measurable by Babylonian standards of success: *more*—more people, more money, more property, more assets, etc.

Christ's kingdom government exists in the tension between leadership authority and the dignifying and elevating of the people of God. It is not a matter of form: committee leadership where the pastor or apostle is under the thumb of the lowest consensus ethic of the people; or set-man leadership, where the people are under a single individual at the top of the hierarchy where no one has real, functional, authority to tell the set man: "*No*, you will not do this or that." Both are extremes. The answer lies in rediscovery of a New Covenant spiritual reality, not swapping one form for the other in an endless cycle of reactionary movements. Spirit-led, Calvary-energized, mutuality of submission is the answer.

It is possible to be strongly congregational in governmental leanings and not be under the influence of "cultural spirits of independence" but merely looking for simple human dignity: *But it is not easy*. It is also possible to have strong executive, authority-type leanings and not inherently abuse people: *But it is not easy.* The answer is in Christ and Him crucified. His cross is where the two irreconcilable qualities of mercy and justice find reconciliation. It will be where congregationalism and set-man authoritarianism find their perfect meeting place. The result will likely be unsatisfying to either extreme.

Authority is defined by responsibility, not privilege. Paul's passion was to give sightedness to people.[11] Because of Whom he had seen, He bore the responsibility of authority to empower others in the same faculty of sight—to see Whom he had seen.[12] The responsibility and sole reason for the exercise of authority in the New Covenant is to facilitate sightedness in the people of God. Sightedness is the inward apprehension of Christ, conformity to that apprehension,[13] and individual empowerment for the world's and the faith community's benefit. To be legitimate, authority must be saturated with New Covenant theology, ethics, methods, and a spirit of empowerment and equalization.

What might this look like structurally? Perhaps the diagrams on the next two pages can graphically sum things up. The arrows represent the flow of authority (*exousia*). A represents an apostle (or any executive leader); B represents other believers or ministers. In the first diagram, authority flows like a substance. In the second diagram, authority is an empowering environment. Hopefully, each graphic can pictorially capture different facets of what I have been trying to say.

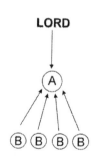

FLAWED AND DANGEROUS

•Authority flows (is given) to the apostle from both the Lord and subordinates (believers, other ministers, etc.)

•Authority "collects" or "resides in an individual, the "apostle."

•Hierarchical

•Class distinction

•Promotes believer dependency

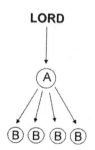

IMPROVED BUT DEFICIENT

•Authority flows from the Lord to the apostle, who then transmits grace to the believer

WEAKNESS:

•The model is still class distinctive, hierarchical and mediatory

•Promotes believer passivity

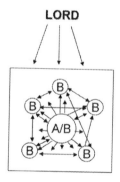

KINGDOM IDEAL

•Authority flows to the community; every individual activated and empowered from the Lord

•The community functions in mutuality, sharing *charis* (grace) and *exousia* (authority)

•The apostle (who is also a believer in the community) has a greater grace endowment and sphere of influence (authority/*exousia*) , therefore, has the greatest mandate, ability, call, and responsibility for sharing empowering grace and authority with others

The flow of kingdom authority.

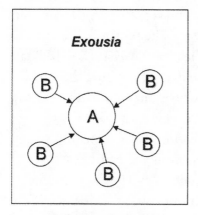

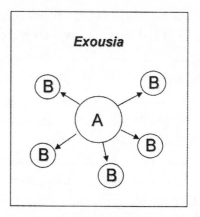

Faulty/False/Dangerous

•Every member "in authority;" empowered, but one way flow

•Authority accumulates in the individual apostle

•Promotes member dependency

Improved, but Deficient

•Every member "in authority;" empowered; rank and endowment acknowledged, but still class distinctive

•Authority does not accumulate individually, is distributive for benefit

•Promotes member passivity, no individual activation; No kingdom mutuality

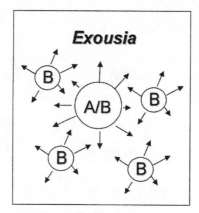

Kingdom Ideal

•Every member "in authority;" empowered, activated, functioning

•The apostle (also a member of the believing community) has greater endowment, therefore, greater sphere of influence and responsibility for divestment

•Mutuality of flow, mutual submission

•Non-hierarchical, non-mediatory

The flow of kingdom authority.

ENDNOTES

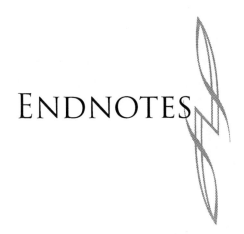

Preface

[1] For those over forty, a cliché from an annoying robot in the campy sixties TV series, *Space Family Robinson*. Who did you want dead most? Mr. Smith or the robot?!

[2] Not taking first-century Semitic culture out of the Scriptures or reading twenty-first-century Western culture into the Scriptures!

[3] Gr. *agapé:* a posture and act of unmerited goodwill.

[4] 1 Corinthians 12–14.

[5] Jeremiah 1:10, for example: four exhortations to tear down, two to build up. A two-to-one ratio of "negative" preaching! You won't get invited to be the guest speaker at the positive-living conference preaching that way!

[6] Adapted from: Wilson, Robert. *Prophecy and Society in Ancient Israel.* Philadelphia: Fortress Press, 1980.

Introduction

[1] John 20:17: "Touch me not": Gr. *háptomai*: Absolutely stop holding me, trying to exert a modifying influence upon me; Zodhiates, Spiros. *The Complete Word Study New Testament*. Chattanooga: AMG Publishers, 1991.

[2] Revelation 3:7.

[3] Isaiah 22:22.

[4] 1 John 2:13: Young men are characterized by overcoming the evil one—combativeness, warfare, fighting.

[5] 1 John 2:13–14.

[6] Matthew 23:24.

[7] *Contradiction*: Direct opposition between statements, conclusions, laws, or principles so that it remains impossible for the statements, conclusions, laws, or principles being compared to both are true at the same time, in the same location, and in the same context. An example would be the people of Jerusalem at one instant concluding that Jesus was not the Messiah because they knew where He came from and at another instant concluding He was not the Messiah because they did know where He came from.

Paradox: An apparent contradiction; something that seems like a contradiction but at least has the possibility of resolution when examined in all possibly existing time, space, and contextual frames of reference. An example would be a man aging only thirty years as he makes a round trip at relativistic velocity to the Andromeda Galaxy while back home the earth would experience the passing of four million years.

Antinomy: Opposition or a contradiction between statements, conclusions, laws, or principles that seem equally logical, reasonable, or necessary. An example would be the Puritan conclusion that both human free will and divine predestination are undeniably true and yet undeniably contradictory.

[8] Refer to any commentary or lexicon.

[9] I will not engage in debate concerning the world in John 3 as being only the elect, other than to say it is a reasonable attempt to try to explain some of the very "tensions" in Scripture I am referring to. Whether it is ultimately correct or not is beyond the scope of this writing.

[10] Refer to Malina, Bruce. J. and Rohrbaugh, Richard L. *Social Science Commentary on the Synoptic Gospels.* Minneapolis: Fortress, 1992; and the *Social Science Commentary on the Gospel of John.* Minneapolis: Fortress, 1998.

[11] Proverbs 10:12, 17:9.

[12] Proverbs 27:5; Luke 17:3.

[13] Isaiah 9:6–7.

[14] Fee, Gordon. *Listening to the Spirit in the Text.* Grand Rapids: Wm. B. Eerdmans Co. and Vancouver, BC: Regents College Publishing, 2000, p. 143.

[15] Ibid., p. 144.

[16] I am aware that there are numbers of groups who would consider themselves as having been apostolic in title or nature for decades, if not centuries. My use herein of the terms *apostolic* and *apostolic renewal* is defined as those teachings and expressions that have emerged within the last ten to fifteen years with emphasis on the restored "offices" of prophet and apostle, with particular emphasis on the "governmental" nature of these ministries.

Chapter 1

[1] For a definition, explanation, and critique of the term "set man," see chapter 7.

[2] Building on what we know to take us beyond what we know.

[3] The Gospel of John is precise in use of the term *believe*. It is never a noun, always a verb. We believe "into" Christ. This is hard for our

minds to grasp. But it means that our faith is: a) active, b) ongoing and progressive, and c) most importantly, has an object, the person of Christ.

[4] I realize many come from "apostolic" traditions with considerable history and would find my terminology odd. By using the term, I am referring to the emergence in the last fifteen to twenty years within charismatic circles of emphasis on the restored office of apostle as well as prophet from Ephesians 4:11–13.

[5] E.g. Allen, Stephen. *Definitions.* Unpublished notes. n.d.

Allen, Stephen. *An Apostolic Teaching,* electronic newsletter, 8/13/05.

Wagner, C. Peter *Churchquake.* Ventura, CA 93003: Regal Publishing. 1999. p. 104 ff. Used by permission.

Cannistraci, David. *Apostles and the Emerging Apostolic Movement.* Ventura: Regal. 1996. p. 155. Used by permission. The first authoritative apostolic quality listed is bringing order.

David, Jonathan. *Apostolic Strategies Affecting Nations,* privately published, 1997. p. 488.

These are but a sample. My issue is not with the fact that apostles bring order. They do. My issue is with essence, method, emphasis, and priority. See chapter 6 of this book.

[6] Allen, Stephen. "An Apostolic Teaching," August 13, 2005, electronic newsletter.

Alley, John. *The Apostolic Revelation.* Rockhampton: Peace Publishing. 2002, pp. 134–135.

[7] Alley, John. *The Apostolic Revelation, p. 134;* David, Jonathan. *Apostolic Strategies,* p. 209

[8] Alley, *The Apostolic Revelation,* p. 134. More on this later.

[9] For example, see Hamon, Bill. *Apostles Prophets and the Coming Moves of God.* Shippensburg: Destiny Image. pp. 151–152.

[10] Homiletics is the science and art of public preaching, speaking, etc. In the Roman church the sermon is called the "homily."

[11] Matthew 5:8.

[12] See the whole book of Hebrews, particularly 7:19, 22, 8:6, 9, etc.

[13] It is the goodness of God that leads us to repentance (Romans 2:4).

[14] See Allen, "An Apostolic Teaching;," Alley, *The Apostolic Revelation;* Bevere, John. *Under Cover.* Nashville: Thomas Nelson, 2001; David, *Apostolic Strategies.*

[15] Though he had authority, he declines to use it. It is significant for our discussion that he uses the term in relationship to a church that was in rebellion, not his norm of operations in all his churches, *and,* he declines to use his authority. Paul refers to the chance to throw his apostolic weight around in 2 Thessalonians 2:5 and again declines to use his authority. This is the Pauline spirit, not the exercise of authority, but the restraint of authority.

[16] 2 Corinthians 12:13–16, 11:9.

[17] 1 Corinthians 9:7-15.

[18] The same issue exists at the pastoral level in a local church.

[19] Cannistraci, *Apostles,* p. 127.

[20] We will deal with some later.

[21] Paul willingly accepted offerings, but he also worked with his hands. My issue is with apostles who put all their eggs in the tithe and offering basket and will not even consider other Scriptures and their implications as if they have a moral and exegetical right to the tithe from other ministers.

[22] Galatians 5:6, First Corinthians 9:11.

[23] Psalm 2.

[24] See Conner, Kevin. *The Church in the New Testament..* Portland: City Christian Publishing, 1989.

Kenney, Carlton, *His Rule in His Church*. Pineville: Morningstar Publishing, 1991, p. 36.

[25] Excerpted from Carlton Kenney, *His Rule in His Church*, p. 36. Emphasis original. Used by permission For more information: www.morningstarministries.org.

[26] Gr. κάινος, qualitatively new, fresh. The New Covenant is not merely new in sequence of time (νέος). It is qualitatively different.

[27] Gr. οὐ κατά: *Strongs Exhaustive Concordance of the New Testament, Thayers Greek Lexicon, Vines Complete Expository Dictionary of the Old and New Testaments* downloaded from e-Sword at: http://www.e-Sword.net, Rick Meyers, 2002; Zodhiates, Spiros. *The Hebrew-Greek Key Study Bible*: AMG publishers. Chattanooga, TN.

[28] The birth, death, burial, resurrection, ascension, glorification of Christ and the outpouring and indwelling of the Holy Spirit in humanity.

[29] This is not the place to deal with issues of sanctification, personal growth, and spiritual maturity.

[30] Marcion was a second-century heretic. He taught that the entire Old Testament was an inferior revelation with no application whatsoever to the believer. His "Scriptures" did not include the Old Testament.

[31] God's righteousness, the Day of the Lord, the holiness of God, the promise and hope of Messiah, etc.

[32] Exodus 18:21.

[33] Without faith it is impossible to please Him (Hebrews 11:6).

[34] Ezekiel 1:5.

[35] Ezekiel 1:16, 10:10, 1:18. The construction of the wheels was as if one wheel were within a wheel, i.e., as if in the wheel a second were inserted at right angles, so that without being turned it could go toward all the four sides: Keil and Delitzsch commentary on the Old Testament; E-Sword.

[36] Ezekiel 1:26.

37 *Keil & Delitzsch Commentary on the Old Testament.* Downloaded from E-Sword.

38 More about this later.

39 Cannistraci, *Apostles*, p. 145. Emphasis is original.

Chapter 2

1 This is particularly true in the so-called Wisdom Books: Proverbs, Ecclesiastes, Job, and to a lesser extent, the Psalms. It is imperative that third-dimensional death and resurrection and New Covenant glasses be worn when a teacher attempts to apply Scripture from these passages. If third-dimension New Covenant realities are not applied, a *quid pro quo* theology will result, which will be inconsistent with the message of grace and the New Covenant. Bad things happen to folks who are doing everything right and good things happen to people who are sinning. Simple Old Covenant dualistic polarities, and much popular success and prosperity teaching based from it, cannot accommodate that the righteous should suffer or the sinner be blessed. Life is a little more complicated than that. The Calvary Act has transformed the cosmos and must influence our interpretation and application of Old Covenant Scriptures.

2 For example, Joel Osteen: "My message is God is a good God. When you live according to his principles that I believe, he wants you to be happy and healthy and whole. It's really a message of encouragement." Quoted in *Investigators: A Look at Evangelist Joel Osteen* on the WXYZ Web site: http://www.wxyz.com/wxyz/ys_investigations/article/0,2132,WXYZ_15949_3927523,00.html. It is really a message of Old Covenant bondage. Where is the hope if you fail to execute one of the principles?

3 When conversion is genuine and Spirit-wrought, not the result of Western psychological techniques. Dr. D. James Kennedy said on one of his television shows that he believes that 75% of Americans in

attendance in churches are not born again. I agree with him, but that would be another book.

[4] I believe in prosperity, biblically defined, not culturally defined by Western, capitalistic, consumerist values.

[5] Frequently, in sermons I have heard in person and on TV.

[6] Hebrews 11:6 says God is the rewarder of those who seek Him, not obey Him. Two important contextual points: a) it is by faith this is done, and b) it refers to those who seek Him out, seek His person, not merely obey His precepts.

[7] Hebrews 11:6

[8] Job 36:11.

[9] Revelation 2:6, 15. Taken from *nikolas/nike*, ruler/victor/conqueror, and *laos*, laity. It is normally a major mistake to do theology from etymology alone. This is a classic case, where assumption and conjecture are made from word definition and roots and may or may not be accurate.

[10] A quaint and thoroughly unbiblical analogy frequently used by leaders when trying to establish strong executive authority in a single individual. The only problem is that, in addition to its lack of exegetical biblicity, our entire faith is based upon belief in a God that exists in three distinct, co-equal, non-hierarchical executive heads! If the creation is based on the image of God, a better understanding of the Trinity might result in a better expression of governmental issues in the Lord's church. Having multiple executives doesn't seem to bother God. Space prohibits a detailed examination of the heretical teaching of subordination in the Godhead, which is currently experiencing a "revival" in some circles of the church.

[11] Ephesians 1:23; Colossians 2:9.

[12] Viola, Frank. *Who is Your Covering?* Present Testimony Ministry, pp. 62–63.

[13] Ephesians 4:11.

[14] Wagner, *Churchquake*, p.259; Wagner, Peter. *Apostles of the City*. Wagner Publications 2000; excerpt from www.globalharvestministries.org, "*The Hypothesis of "Pastor-Apostles.*" Cannistraci, David. *Apostles*, p. 163. Fairness requires I mention that David includes a moderating exemption that apostles do not "always" attract large numbers, but the underlying premise remains.

[15] Rumble, Don. *Apostolic and Prophetic Foundations*. Clinton Corners: The Attic Press, p. 145.

[16] The biblical mandate concerning being apt to teach has been culturally interpreted as meaning having pulpit expression and persona. You can pastor and not have a pulpit presence, though this is hard to fathom in our culture. We "pay" for preaching, not pastoring, in our culture.

[17] *Semite* is a term used to describe people from the East in a general sense or more specifically the Middle East. Being Semitic means having an "Eastern" worldview rather than "Western."

[18] For a detailed explanation see Malina, Bruce J. and Rohrbaugh, Richard L. *The Social Science Commentary on the Synoptic Gospels* and *The Social Science Commentary on the Gospel of John*. Minneapolis: Augsburg Fortress, 1992.

[19] Unless invited by the community to do so or invited by a superior patron.

[20] Cultural biases and eisegesis in our definitions of many biblical words are covered in chapter 4 of this book.

[21] I will use this term throughout this book to describe Christ's incarnation, death, burial, resurrection, ascension, glorification, and outpouring of the Holy Spirit on the Day of Pentecost.

[22] The same act, the pouring out of the Christ-spirit on Pentecost, both elevates the *doulos* slave/servant and brings low the master/ruler. Joel 2; Acts 2; Matthew 20:26–27, Philemon.

[23] Galatians 3:28; 1 Peter 2:9. Even the slave is free and made a king.

[24] Mark 10:44.

[25] Unless they were dealing with issues of self-hate, false humility, psychological and religious self-flagellation for perceived deficiencies.

[26] Gr. *diakonein*, service, ministry; *literally*, waiting on tables.

[27] Honor must flow in a cycle of mutuality to be legitimate. Leaders who serve well are to be counted worthy of double honor, the least member in the body is to be counted the most honorable.

[28] Luke 16:8.

[29] Non-congregational government, a high set-man ethic, unelected presbyters/bishops rule.

[30] Sheep do not discipline pastors; pastors discipline pastors. Manuel Gutierrez quoted in Wagner, *Churchquake*, p. 100.

[31] Out of the abundance of the heart the mouth speaks.

[32] Some believe that possessing both attributes in a high degree of effectiveness might describe the interior psychology of someone functioning in, or called to, an apostolic dimension; that possessing both qualities/gifts is what distinguishes someone with a trans-local apostolic ministry from a local church pastor. An interesting and perhaps accurate observation for which there is no definitive biblical confirmation one way or the other.

[33] Taken from *Beyond all Limits* by Bill Bright and James O. Davies. Copyright 2000. New Life Publications, Orlando, FL. Used by permission, All rights reserved.

[34] Rumble, *Apostolic and Prophetic Foundations*, p. 132.

Chapter 3

[1] Romans 13:1, from the *Message* by Eugene Peterson. Downloaded from e-Sword at: http://www.esword.net, Rick Meyers, 2002.

[2] Romans 13:1 KJV.

³ Isaiah 9:7.

⁴ Matthew 20:25–26. We will examine this verse in detail later when we discuss spiritual fatherhood.

⁵ Over twenty years ago, I listened to an audiotape by Rick Godwin on this subject. It impacted me greatly at the time, and I have no doubt that a good bit of my presentation herein is residual effect of that message. As I long ago lost the tape (I remember it vaguely as perhaps coming from James Robison's ministry) and do not know whether the content was ever put formally in print by Brother Godwin, I can but give this acknowledgment herein and ask indulgence.

⁶ Philippians 2:1–11. Because He embraced death, He was invested with a name and rank that requires universal obedience and honor. It is so important to note that even the Son of God Himself did not demand or require honor from His position as the Son. Only after He tasted death and resurrection was He given, endowed, and crowned with a name above all others to whom every knee shall bow. Many leaders in the church think they are entitled to honor from subordinates simply because of their position—you honor the position, not the man. Tasting death and resurrection life for others establishes you, not your position, office, or rank in the body of Christ, as one to whom honor is due.

⁷ 2 Peter 1:19; Hebrews 1:2.

⁸ For an excellent presentation of the importance of having a worldview framework for Christian thought, I highly recommend Pearcy, Nancy. *Total Truth*. Wheaton: Crossway, 2004.

⁹ Jeremiah 5:31. A corrupt ruling class, a corrupt prophetic class, and a compliant people were and are required for dysfunctional and low-order Christianity to take root. It is not just a "leadership" issue.

¹⁰ Paul's specific mandate and burden was to make all humanity see what is the fellowship of the mystery (Ephesians 3:9). John the Baptist's

ministry was to point out, make clear and recognizable the Lamb of God. These are prophetic functions.

11 I am not talking about the spirit of the accuser that frequently masquerades under "honest questions."

12 Matthew 22:21; Mark 12:17.

13 The issue of pacifism is beyond the scope of this present writing.

14 In every generation there are trends that come through the body of Christ that are distractions to the simple gospel of Christ and Him crucified. These are issues that are perhaps inferentially, but not directly, supported by Scripture, to which preachers begin to emphasize and expect conformity. The interested reader is referred to the author's text, *The Silent Killers of Faith*, available from the author or Destiny Image Publishing, for a more thorough presentation.

15 1 Corinthians 6:12, 10:23.

16 This either means that thinking and methods like this are more widespread than we would like to believe, or I am incredibly unlucky!

17 I use the term reservedly.

18 1 Corinthians 11:16.

Chapter 4

1 Libertinism: a philosophy of no restraint.

2 Word definitions alone are inadequate for a complete base of instruction, but they are a starting place.

3 Definitional resources include *Strong's Exhaustive Concordance*, *Thayer's Concordance*, *Robertson's Word Pictures of the New Testament*, *The Hebrew Greek Key Study Bible*, *Vines Expository Dictionary*, Bauer, Arndt and Gingrich, *A Greek-English Lexicon of the New Testament*.

4 Wagner, *Churchquake*. p.105.

5 Alley, *The Apostolic Revelation*.

6 See 2 Thessalonians 2:6 for an example of the Pauline spirit. The King James Version says "burdensome"; it means to bring pressure to bear. In our common language it means to "throw one's weight around."

7 Onesimus was a runaway slave of Philemon's, and in their culture this was a capital offense.

8 1 Corinthians 7:25, also, *epitagē*—authoritative injunction/commandment—Paul distinguishes his role as leader from his role as oracle of God.

9 Gnosticism was one of the first heretical teachings the apostles had to face. It is an eclectic system of spirituality based on secret knowledge, rites of initiation, ascending orders of spiritual beings, and a stark duality between the earthly and material realm and the heavenly and spiritual realm. Gnostics believed all matter was evil, belonging to the fallen order, and only "spirit" constituted pure reality. A lot of popular TV preaching in charismatic circles is Gnostic and pseudo-Gnostic.

10 Bevere, John. *Under Cover.* Nashville: Thomas Nelson. 2001.

11 Titus 1:10–16.

12 Titus 1:12.

13 I use the term as it is commonly and unfortunately used in charismatic circles. Technically, there is only one "revelation," the Scriptures. There are many illuminations of the one Revelation. I encourage folks everywhere to eliminate the use of the term *revelation* when referring to subjective impressions and insights into the Word.

14 Wagner, et. al.

15 See chapter 7 of this book.

16 1 Corinthians 1:12.

17 John 21:15–17; Acts 20:28–29: "feeding" being a shepherding metaphor for care, extended to protecting against enemies of the flock, not ruling the flock with authority.

18 Hebrews 13:17.

[19] Colossians 3:20–22.

[20] The New Testament does use it in the Gospels, but the status of the disciples' "faith" and "conversion status" prior to the resurrection is a debatable proposition. This we do know, Pentecost accomplished a change in and through the apostles. They were not the same men.

[21] Nyland, Ann. *Papyri, Women, and Word Meaning in the New Testament.* Priscilla Papers, Volume 17, Number 4. Fall 2003.

[22] The Seventy: It refers to the Hebrew Old Testament Scriptures translated into Greek done by seventy scholars.

[23] Mickelson, Berkley and Alvera. *The Head of the Epistles.* "Christianity Today," February 20, 1981.

[24] Cervin, Richard S. *Does kephalē (head) Mean Source or Authority Over in Greek Literature?: A Rebuttal:* article provided by Christians for Biblical Equality, Minneapolis, MN.

[25] Refer to Cervin, Mickelson, Cunningham, and Hamilton, and many others within the biblical egalitarian movement.

[26] Cunningham, Loren and Hamilton, David Joel. *Why Not Women?* Seattle: YWAM Publishing, 2000. p. 163.

[27] Though normally a sound mentor in the things of the deeper Christian life, Watchman Nee does have some latent strains of legalism, and his Trinitarian doctrine in his classic, *Spiritual Authority* (reprinted as *Authority and Submission*), is categorically unsound. I do not recommend his book on this topic. It is oppressive in spirit. Nee, Watchman. *Authority and Submission*, Anaheim: Living Stream Ministry, 1988, p. 41–42.

[28] The Scriptures that refer to Christ as inferior to the Father or subordinate to the Father are speaking of His role in the incarnation as humanity's Redeemer for the purposes of accomplishing our redemption. In His eternality as the Logos of God, He is God, equal to God, and there is no subordinancy. The creed accurately reads: "God the Father, God the Son, and God the Holy Spirit." Our authority

doctrine in the church would improve in direct proportion to better understanding of apostolic teaching concerning the Trinity.

²⁹ Woodroffe, Noel. *The Present Reformation of the Church*. Miami: EMI Publications. 2000. p. 9.

³⁰ See Cunningham and Hamilton, 159–175.

³¹ Matthew 20:25-26.

³² Morris, Leon, editor. *Tyndale NT Commentary, Revised Edition*, Reprinted. :Intervarsity. 2000, 152.

³³ I could not disagree more strongly with John Bevere's (and others') assertion, that submission is given to the office, not the person, and that in the presence of ungodly or unworthy authority, the believer's correct response is silent submission. The elders who rule *well* are counted worthy (1 Timothy 5:17). The basis for the "honor the office" teaching is from the Old Covenant stories. The bulk of Bevere's book, *Under Cover*, is filled with Old Testament character stories and personal anecdotes. There is very little post-Pentecost, New Testament exposition. There is a reason for that. The New Testament teaches that if someone is overtaken in a fault, we rebuke them, not submit to them (Luke 17:3). The reason for the Old Covenant deference on this matter is because the anointing rested singularly on individuals. That is no longer the case. The post-Pentecost, Spirit-age has put everyone on equal footing. The least among us is worthy of the more honor, and the least can rebuke the greatest, when it is necessary. Pneumatic (Spirit) equalization is not the same thing as a spirit of democracy that Bevere and others so seem to dread. Someone could argue that Paul is submissive to unworthy authority in Acts 23, 25, and 26 when he appears before the high priest, Felix, and Agrippa. In Acts 23, Paul apologizes for the insult (whited wall) he used toward the high priest, not the fact the he confronts ungodly authority with their ungodliness. I would also say that he is simply following the injunction to honor civic authority and that honor is not equivalent with absolute

compliance. None of the individuals were within the community of faith-they were not "brothers." This is a situation where what applies "outside the covenant community" does not translate "exactly" into the covenant community: the general value system does, but the exact implementation does not. Space prohibits fully explaining the difference between "in-group" and "out-group" ethical obligations in the Semitic/Mediterranean/biblical/first-century world, except to say, that in their culture, silence in the presence of unworthy authority was not equivalent to submission but rather an insult. Other cultural issues also have bearing on the subject.

[34] Acts 20:28–29. The King James Version unfortunately translates the Greek preposition, *en* (meaning "in or among"), as *over* in this passage. The hierarchical bias shows again. The elders are not "over" the flock; they are "in" or "among" the flock. Refer to any competent Greek grammar in the preposition section to verify this.

[35] Matthew 20:25.

[36] Viola, Frank. *Who is Your Covering?* p. 36.

[37] See chapter five of this text.

Chapter 5

[1] It was a major characteristic of the Discipleship Movement of the 1970s.

[2] Wagner, *Churchquake*, p. 98.

[3] 2 Corinthians 6, 4, 12:12, 15.

[4] Terminology we can overlook but should likely change. I recommend not using it because of its contaminated implications.

[5] Alley, *The Apostolic Revelation*, p. 134

[6] Ibid.

[7] Philippians 3:10.

[8] See Bevere, *Under Cover*, throughout the text.

[9] Not from a spirit of independence but from integrated psychological wholeness and authentic personhood in Him and interdependence with one another.

[10] Clayton, C.W. *Accountable Men.* Hagerstown: Covenant Printing. n.d., p. 5.

[11] Jeremiah 5:31.

[12] Alley, *The Apostolic Revelation.* pp. 39, 83, 134, 135, and 157. I have noticed a commonality among some called apostles. They consider themselves to be gifted in a "revelatory way." Often, they are exegetically weak. They tend to teach from their inspirations *about* Scripture rather than the exegesis *of* Scripture, relying on proof texts here and there to supplement what they believe they have received by "revelation." In the case of Bro. Alley's book, though certainly not limited to him, it is especially true. Throughout the book, he regularly teaches from his dreams, visions, and subjective impressions of the Lord's voice. This is the curse of charismaticdom, a formula for disaster and a completely unsound basis for apostolic doctrine. Dreams and visions are meant for personal encouragement and edification and, at times, guidance, but they are not the basis for apostolic doctrine, nor to be the basis to conform other's kingdom behaviors, thinking, etc. I am really grieved on this matter. Every group or organization that has started on this road has ended up in the historical ash heap—without exception.

[13] Ibid., p. 135.

[14] Kelly, John. *Words from a Father. The Networker* (April 1997), p.3.; quoted in Wagner, *Churchquake.*

[15] Bevere, *Under Cover.* p.89.

[16] David, Jonathan. *Apostolic Strategies Affecting Nations.* Malaysia. Privately Published. 1997, pp. 209–210.

[17] Ibid., p. 209.

[18] Ibid., pp. 209–210.

[19] Bevere, *Under Cover*, p. 227.

[20] Cannistraci, David. *Five Signs of a Solid Spiritual Covering*. "Charisma Magazine," July 2005, p. 54. Of all the authors I have read on the subject, Bro. Cannistraci's presentation of the topic is the healthiest I have seen as he defines covering by prayer and relationship and lists many legitimate pitfalls to avoid (some mentioned in this text). I just wish the term *covering* would go away because of its unfortunate implications and misuse, including the image in the article of an umbrella as the instrument of "covering."

[21] Ibid.

[22] Ibid.

[23] Ibid., p. 55

[24] Ibid.

[25] Stephen G. Allen, unpublished message.

[26] Rumble, Apostolic *and Prophetic Foundations*. p. 83.

[27] Ibid., 83.

[28] Ibid., 83.

[29] Ibid., 84.

[30] Fee, Gordon. *The First Epistle to the Corinthians: The NIV International Commentary on the New Testament*. Grand Rapids: Eerdmans, 1987. p. 507.

[31] Ibid., p. 508.

[32] Ibid., p. 512.

[33] Ibid., p. 521.

[34] Luke 23:45; Mark 15:38; Matthew 27:51.

[35] 2 Corinthians 3:14.

[36] See Bevere, *Under Cover*.

[37] This text is likely to get me enough enemies to last a while, so I respectfully decline to get in on the hymn vs. choruses melee!

38 Bevere openly endorses this thinking, explicitly stating that if a believer disobeys he/she is under a curse and will be punished with hardship, sickness, or some other form of affliction (duly quoting an Old Covenant verse!), and if you obey you are blessed. See *Under Cover*, pp. 10, 11, 61, 77, and throughout. This is nothing other than Old Covenant Deuteronomic thinking: If you do well, you will be blessed, and if you don't, you will be punished. Both in spirit and content this is far from New Covenant understanding. Space prohibits a digression into New Covenant theology.

39 Psalm 103:12.

40 Roberts, A. and Donaldson, J. eds. *The Anti Nicene Fathers*. Vol. 1. Chapter Five, pp. 101–102; Christian Life Electronic Library, Columbus, GA.

41 Rumble, *Apostolic and Prophetic Foundations*, p. 81.

Chapter 6

1 No gender limitations are implied in the usage of this biblical terminology.

2 Allen, Stephen. *An Apostolic Teaching*. 8/13/05. Electronic newsletter.

3 Rumble, *Apostolic Foundations*, p. 70.

4 Romans 8:19.

5 John 20:17.

6 There is no issue with honoring our leaders. The problem is one of degree and balance. If honor flows only to leadership ministries and "spiritual fathers" rather than honor flowing one to another in the community in the spirit of mutuality, the legitimate principle of honor becomes corrupted.

7 Mandatory in some circles as "honoring leaders."

[8] 1 Corinthians 12:23–24. The Scriptures are clear. Honor is not to be bestowed upon rank; they don't need it. Honor is to be bestowed upon those who "lack" and whom we would consider the least honorable. The apostolic movement is dishonorable in its policies of honor!

[9] 1 Peter 2:17.

[10] Exell, Joseph and Spence H.D.M, eds. *The Pulpit Commentary*: McClean: Macdonald Publishing, n.d., p. 397.

[11] Albert Barnes Commentary on Matthew 23.

[12] Keener, Craig. *IVP Bible Background Commentary of the New Testament,* 1993; Electronic Edition STEP files. 1999. Parsons Technology.

[13] Refer to Malina, Bruce. J. and Rohrbaugh, Richard L. *Social Science Commentary on the Synoptic Gospels.* Minneapolis: Fortress, 1992.

[14] The supposed principle is that an individual must serve faithfully in another man's ministry before he or she can be legitimately released in to their own. While learning servanthood is undeniably a kingdom virtue, I would like to point out that the context of this is talking about relationship to commerce, money, and mammon. It says nothing about ministerial protocols. Applying this passage to ministerial dynamics is a *huge inference*.

[15] Quoted from Chuck Clayton, Apostolic Resources Ministries, Versailles, Indiana. Verbal conversation, used by permission.

[16] What would Jesus do?

[17] Judas

[18] "After some time, I came to realize that, in Christ that I was providing a spiritual covering for the people." Alley, p. 135.

[19] Philemon 10; 2 Timothy 2:1; Titus 1:4.

[20] Hanby, Mark. *You Have Not Many Fathers*. Shippensburg: Destiny Image, 1996. p. xxv.

21 Advertisements in some charismatic Christian magazines offer "spiritual fathering and apostolic covering" for a monthly fee. This practice is an abomination.

22 Hamlet.

23 Wagner, *Churchquake.* The major premise of the book is the apostolic as defined by authority.

24 Allen, Stephen, *An Apostolic Teaching*, 8/13/05, email newsletter.

25 The term *ministry* is so culturally contaminated by the connotation of professional clergy that it is almost useless.

26 I am indebted to Frank Viola's work, *Who is Your Covering?*, for this compilation. See pp. 114–115. Also, Hebrews was likely not authored by Paul.

27 In Acts 20:28, it is unfortunate that the King James Version translated the Greek preposition *en* as *over*. It does not mean that. It means "in or among." The Greek preposition for *over* is *epi*. The correct emphasis for a leader or elder is not their status as "over" the flock but from "among" the flock completely in sympathy with "ye are all brethren" of Matthew 23:8.

28 Thysman, Raymond, *Communauté et directives éthiques; la catéchèse de Matthieu* (1974), 84 quote in Bruner, Frederick, *Matthew: A Commentary*, p. 437.

29 Refer to any of the texts dealing with the apostolic listed in the bibliography herein. They do a good job on the basics.

30 Allen, Stephen, *Defintions*, a worksheet handout, n.d. The first quality listed is spiritual authority. Wagner, *Churchquake*, "an apostle is someone who has extraordinary authority." p. 105.

31 Ibid.

32 Rumble, *Apostolic and Prophetic Foundation*, p. 23.

33 Ibid., p. 51.

[34] 1 Corinthians 3:11: Christ and Him crucified. There is no other foundation.

[35] The belief that certain functions and offices in the church were lost through neglect or by ecclesiastical design and that part of the "last day" move of God is to restore all of the lost offices and functions.

[36] Rumble, *Apostolic Foundations*, p. 51.

[37] Kelly, John. Informational packet for Antioch Churches and ministries, n.p., n.d., cited in Wagner, *Churchquake*, p. 113.

[38] Calvin, John, *Institutes of the Christian Religion*. Book IV, Chapter 8; downloaded from e-Sword at: http://www.esword.net, Rick Meyers, 2002.

[39] For expansion of this thought, please refer to Viola, Frank, *Who is Your Covering*, pp. 44–45.

[40] Milam, Donald. "Who is Head of the Church?" Radical Grace Communiqué #24, 2/11/2004; electronic newsletter.

Chapter 7

[1] Conner, Kevin, *The Church in the New Testament*. Portland: City Christian Publishing. 1989. pp. 204–205. Used by Permission.

[2] To a lesser extent, presidents, though in a representative republic he can be stopped. If folks want to use this metaphor for supporting set man government in the church, let's follow it all the way.

[3] He quotes a scripture from Acts 7, quoting an Old Testament story.

[4] See Bevere, *Under Cover* for typical adjuring.

[5] Adapted from Viola, Frank. *Who is Your Covering?* pp. 32–33.

[6] I am aware that in 2 John the apostle addresses "the elect lady" and her children, the church. This is a problematic verse. If it is written to a literal elect lady, it brings up the whole issue of women in leadership, which I will kindly sidestep at this writing. However, if it is a metaphor for the church as a whole, then it just adds more evidence

supporting the concept of addressing the church, a problem for the set-man mediator theology.

[7] Ephesians 4:13.

[8] Intimacy defined as obedience, not devotional and emotional highs. "If you love me (intimacy), keep my commandments" (John 15:10).

[9] Matthew 25:14–30 and Luke 19:11–27.

[10] 1 Corinthians 12:7, 11.

[11] Gill, John, *Exposition of the Entire Bible*, E-Sword. Any other commentary will indicate the same.

[12] Rumble, Don. *The Latter Day Glory*. El Cajon: Christian Services Network. 2004, p 66.

[13] Paul's apostolic mandate was to enable others to see (Ephesians 3:8–11).

[14] Genesis 11:4–9.

[15] Paul clearly employed strategic thinking in his missionary and church-planting endeavors.

[16] Latin: "the essential thing, the thing upon which all other depends, the essential ingredient."

[17] Philippians 1:16–18; Mark 9:38–40.

[18] Matthew 7:23.

Chapter 8

[1] There are different ways to view the matter of calling. At one level it can refer to the foreordained, sovereign, and irrevocable decision of God toward an individual that abides on him/her from cradle to grave. This is not what I mean. When it comes to leaders/elders I use the term to refer to the divine initiation toward and within an individual that energizes and activates individual will/desire, which in turn spurs to action to complete a divinely assigned task. Eldership is

not a calling in the former definition, but it is in the latter. Being an elder or a leader in a positional/function/task sense is not necessarily an irrevocable lifetime calling. Individuals can "step in and out" of being an "elder." For example, an elder can be removed, resign, retire, or take a sabbatical. Also an individual may be an elder in church A, but should he geographically relocate, the same individual is not automatically an elder in church B because of a residing "call" upon his life "to be an elder." Much local church conflict could be avoided if this distinction were understood.

[2] 1 Corinthians 9:16.

[3] 2 Corinthians 2:14–16.

[4] John 6:41–58: "except you eat . . ." Psalm 34:8.

[5] Chambers, Oswald, *My Utmost for His Highest*, October 18; downloaded from e-Sword at: http://www.esword.net, Rick Meyers, 2002.

[6] 1 Peter 5:1–2. He was an apostle and an elder.

[7] Thayers, Strongs, Complete Word Study New Testament.

[8] Acts 20:28.

[9] 1 Timothy 3:1.

[10] Ibid.

[11] I am not implying masculine limitations when using masculine pronouns; however, since this work is likely to irritate enough folks on its own, I will pass on engaging in the "women-in-ministry" debate.

[12] Marital dynamics can vary as widely as the trees in the forest and still be "biblical." It is very dangerous to project cultural psychotherapeutic value systems on to one another's marriages and deem someone's marriage as "deficient" as individuals because they may not share the same emotional value system you do. The biblical measuring stick is precise and limited: sexual fidelity, mutual love, (not the popular "romance" advocated by many contemporary Christian marriage specialists) honor

and submission. More than this is unwarranted cultural projection and expectation into the passage.

[13] Malina and Rohrbaugh, *Social Science Commentaries of the Synoptics and John.*

[14] Ibid. This reality will put most fundamentalists over the edge.

Chapter 9

[1] Rushdie, Salman. Cited in *Uncle John's Bathroom Reader*, 15th edition, Ashland: Bathroom Readers Press, 2002, p. 265.

[2] Genesis 3:5.

[3] In an American or Western context, you could substitute *celebrity* for *specialist*.

[4] Payne, Leanne. Pastoral Care Ministries, Summer 2005 newsletter, p. 2. Payne believes (and I agree) that the prophetic movement (wait until she catches a whiff of the "apostolic movement") will dwarf Jehovah's Witnesses and the Mormons in cultic dimension if not soon corrected, hence, my passion in this book.

[5] This is a real and present danger in the "father-son" message—a inner psychological posture of eternal childishness in a bad sense that is easily interpreted as: covering, sonship, accountability, submission to authority, etc.

[6] Payne, p. 9. sub-article by, Pertuit, Mark. "False Prophets or Genuine Prophetic Leadership?"

[7] Ibid., see pages 8–9.

[8] John 3:16 and the entire gospel record.

[9] Philippians 2:6–11.

[10] Matthew 10:39; Mark 8:35; Luke 9:24.

[11] Ephesians 3:9, 18–19.

[12] Seeing is an inclusive metaphor or understanding meaning "initial sight, accompanied with understanding of, and conformity to, the object of sight."

[13] Obedience, transformation into His image, Christlikeness.

RECOMMENDED READING AND WORKS CITED

Alley, John K. *The Apostolic Revelation: The Reformation of the Church.* Rockhampton: Peace Publishing, 2002.

Anderson, Neil and Mylander, Charles. *Setting Your Church Free.* Ventura: Regal Books, 1994.

Arterburn, Stephen, and Felton, Jack. *Toxic Faith: Understanding and Overcoming Religious Addiction.* Nashville: Oliver Nelson, 1991.

Bevere, John, *Under Cover.* Nashville: Thomas Nelson, 2001.

Blue, Ken. *Healing Spiritual Abuse.* Downer's Grove: Intervarsity Press, 1993.

Bright, Bill and Davies, James O. *Beyond All Limits.* Orlando: New Life Productions, 2000.

Bruner, Frederick. *Matthew: A Commentary.* Grand Rapids: Eerdmans, 1990.

Cannistraci, David. *Apostles and the Emerging Apostolic Movement.* Ventura: Renew, 1996.

Chambers, Oswald. *My Utmost for His Highest.* Westwood: Barbour and Company, 1963.

Clayton, Chuck. *Accountable Men.* Hagerstown: Covenant Printing. n.d.

Conner, Kevin J. *The Church in the New Testament*. Portland: City Christian Publishing: 1989.

Crosby, Stephen. *Silent Killers of Faith*. Shippensburg: Treasure House. 2004.

Cunningham, Loren and Hamilton, David Joel. *Why Not Women?* Seattle: YWAM. 2000.

Damazio, Frank. *The Making of a Leader*. Portland: Bible Temple Publishing, 1988.

David, Jonathan. *Apostolic Strategies Affecting Nations*. Self-published: Malaysia, 1997.

Exell, Joseph and Spence H.D.M, eds. *The Pulpit Commentary*: McClean: Macdonald Publishing, n.d.

Farnsworth, Kirk E. *Wounded Workers: Recovering From Heartache in the Workplace and Church*. Mukilteo: Winepress Publishing, 1998.

Fee, Gordon. *Listening to the Spirit in the Text*. Grand Rapids: Eerdmans, 2000.

———. NIV *Commentary on the New Testament, The First Epistle to the Corinthians*. Grand Rapids: Eerdmans, 1987.

Giles, Kevin. *The Trinity and Subordinationism: The Doctrine of God and the Contemporary Gender Debate*. Downers Grove: IVP, 2002.

Hamon, W. *Apostles and Prophets and the Coming Moves of God*. Shippensburg: Destiny Image, 1997.

Hanby, Mark. *You have Not Many Fathers*. Shippensburg: Destiny Image, 1996.

Kenny, Carlton. *His Rule in His Church*. Pineville: Morningstar Publications, 1991.

Nee, Watchman. *Authority and Submission*. Anaheim: Living Stream Ministry, 1988.

Noble, John. *The Shaking*. London: Monarch Books, 2002.

Payne, Leanne. Pastoral Care Ministries. Summer 2005 newsletter.

Roberts, Alexander and Donaldson, James, eds. *Ante-Nicene Fathers*. *Vol. I*. Peabody: Hendrickson, 1995. 10 vols.

Rumble, Donald. *Apostolic and Prophetic Foundations*: *Giving the Lord back His Church*: Clinton Corners: Attic Studio Press, 1996.

———. *The Latter Day Glory*. El Cajon: Christian Services Network. 2004.

Viola, Frank. *Who is Your Covering*. Third edition. Present Testimony Ministry. 2001.

Wagner, C. Peter. *Churchquake*. Ventura: Regal, 1999.

Wagner, C. Peter. *Churchquake—Apostles of the City.* The New Apostolic Reformation, 10 Dec. 2002, <http://www.globalharvest.org>

Wilson, Robert. *Prophecy and Society in Ancient Israel*. Philadelphia: Fortress, 1980.

Woodroffe, Noel. *The Present Reformation of the Church*. Miami: EMI Publications, 2000.

LaVergne, TN USA
02 September 2010
195593LV00001B/50/A